SPECIAL MESSAGE TO LOVING PARENTS ❤

Hello! I am so glad that you are holding my book in your hands! I am especially happy that our lives as parents—yours and mine—have crossed. I know that you are someone committed to your baby, or this kind of book would not have attracted your attention. You want to give your baby every opportunity to be the best that he/she can be. Me, too! That's why I wrote this book of practical strategies. I want to make a lasting difference in young lives.

I Love You, Baby was written for expectant mothers, fathers, and siblings. It is designed to help parents understand the need for giving the newborn daily verbal encouragement for healthy psychological development. As parents we wouldn't think of starving Baby's body, but many infants are psychologically starved. Not because parents do not care, but because we lack the tenacity needed to provide positive daily affirmations. Busy with diapering, feeding, soothing, nursing illnesses, dressing, and bathing, we don't seem to find time to squeeze even one more thing into the day. And yet, we have this anxious, nagging feeling that something is being left undone, unsaid, incomplete.

Because of the brilliant works of Eric Berne, Alice Miller, Erick Erikson, John Bradshaw, and others, millions of people are beginning to understand how the child develops and how unmet childhood needs later contaminate the adult self. People buy self-help books, seek therapy, and attend workshops to aid

their recovery. However, no books are being published that teach us how to raise psychologically healthy children. Instead of waiting until children are adults that need fixing, why not get newborns started on a positive, warm, nourishing path so they can grow to be functional and filled with self-worth?

I Love You, Baby was written to give parents daily words to speak to the newborn. Not only are the words there, but the training that it takes to help a parent become a positive, loving parent every day is there! Psychologists say that after we do something seventy-seven times, it becomes a habit—we own it—it becomes a part of us. Daily affirmations are the perfect format because lessons that are practiced and reinforced over and over for a long period of time are the lessons that we master.

The daily affirmations herein will give you positive stepping stones along the path of healthy parenting with each and every day's reading. And there is more! There are nursery rhymes, Bible verses (NKJV), famous sayings to cheer you, parenting tips, a list of Baby's milestones, and growth charts. You get all of this in one book—the book you are holding—*I Love You, Baby*. Enjoy!

A Note to Families ❤

Today's nuclear family can also be an isolated family. This and other modern societal factors create many challenges and insecurities for those of us raising children. In many cases, a mother or father has only a few precious hours with their baby between "pick-up time" and bedtime. Now, more than ever, our children need to be provided with an abiding trust in their caregiver's benevolence and a basic trust in their own goodness. The reflection we see of ourselves as human beings in the mirror held by today's media is frightening. Families spend hours and hours in front of a noisy box that presents humankind at its most ridiculous, aggressive, and lascivious.

As parents, we have the power to hold up a positive mirror to ourselves and our children, one that will reflect an essence in each of us that is deeply good, courageous, and divine. These gentle, loving daily affirmations will provide you with just such a mirror, a spiritual tool. Full of love and appreciation, these concise affirmations, inspirational quotes, and parenting tips will provide comfort and sow the seeds of possibility for both parent and child.

You have wonderful days ahead! Parenting a newborn will provide the amazing proof of the consistent building process that life is intended to be. Your baby, in all probability, will stretch you to your limits both physically and emotionally. Have faith that you will be a better, stronger, and more serene person because of the love and care you will give to this tiny person.

How to Use this Book ❤

You may read these daily affirmations to Baby any time during the day; however, it is highly recommended that you read and reread them to Baby while you are feeding him/her. Feeding time provides more than good nutrition for your newborn. It is an opportunity to hold, cuddle, and make eye contact with this precious person. It is a special time during which you can talk to Baby and tell him/her how special he/she is. This time will bring you and your child closer together and foster strong bonding. Keep this book by the rocking chair or other place where you sit and hold Baby when feeding him/her. While speaking these affirmations to your baby, treat the tiny one with love. Be affectionate. Give plenty of physical contact through hugging, kissing, playing, and cuddling. Talk to Baby in a soft, gentle voice. Smile. Relax. Trust in your own ability to be a powerful force for good in this tiny person's life!

Begin with the affirmation written especially for the day your baby is born. If it isn't exactly what you want to say to welcome your baby, you may want to write your own birthday affirmation. Then, begin on the appropriate day and read the daily affirmation three to seven times each day. When you see the word, "**Baby**," substitute your baby's name. Humans, especially children, love the sound of their own name. Say your baby's name many times each day.

When referring to Baby, I have sometimes chosen to alternate masculine and feminine pronouns. It was the only practical way to avoid "he/she," "his/hers," etc., which often became awkward because it appeared many times in each paragraph. Feel free to change the affirmations to suit your particular needs. For example, you may want to substitute the word, "we," for "I," and present the affirmations for the whole family. Fathers and siblings may want to read the affirmations to Baby, too. Make sure that each affirmation is clearly what you want to say. If it is not the message you genuinely want to communicate, substitute another affirmation or make up your own. There is nothing magical about the affirmations in this book. After you use them for a while, you will soon be adapting them and creating your own affirmations for your unique baby.

The important thing to remember is to use them! If you forget for a few days or weeks, don't give up. Go back and begin on the appropriate day. Take advantage of the empty space to journal on most pages. Note each of Baby's milestones. Record your feelings and special thoughts about mothering. These baby days will make the memories that will fill you with joy for the rest of your life.

Happy birthday,
Happy, happy, birthday!

I am glad you are here, **Baby**. We gave you the name, _____. I was awed by the first sight of you. Giving birth was an extraordinary experience. We both had to work very hard. You were courageous. You wanted to come into this world, and now you are here to begin your life. I am glad you are here. I cherish you. I have been waiting for you to be born. I am glad you are a (boy/girl). I have prepared a special place for you. I will take you to the special place soon. I will support you in all that you do. You are treasured. I love you, **Baby**!

I saw three ships come sailing by,
On New Year's Day in the morning.

Nursery Rhyme

I welcome and nurture the changes and growth I see in you each day, **Baby**. You can trust in the goodness and strength I lovingly offer you. You are a special gift from Heavenly Father.

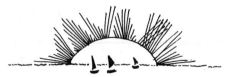

Where did you come from, baby dear?
Out of the everywhere into the here.

George MacDonald

·✦·══◗ ◖══·✦·

You are a great treasure, **Baby**. From the moment I first held you in my arms, my world has been richer. I know how valuable you are, and I love watching you become the person you will be.

You are growing and learning at exactly the right speed, **Baby**. There is no hurry to get anywhere other than where we are. Where we are is perfect for you, and perfect for me.

Even babies need applause. Praise Baby at each new learning step. Smile and let your face show that you are happy to watch her progress. Be patient and enjoy each milestone of Baby's progression.

I enjoy gently stroking your head and patting your back, **Baby**. I like to rock you and sing you to sleep. I look forward to the special times we share.

Often when a baby cries uncontrollably, rubbing the stiff little back will help him relax. Stroking Baby defines his body for him. It helps him learn where his body begins and ends. It teaches him that he is an individual human being.

Rock-a-Bye, baby, thy cradle is green;
Father's a nobleman, mother's a queen.

Nursery Rhyme

———

Do you like your bed, **Baby**? It is a bed just for you. It will support you so that you can rest and feel refreshed many times each day. My arms will support you and hold you when you need comforting. The world is a safe place, and the planet welcomes you, **Baby**.

It takes a long time to bring
excellence to maturity.

Publilius Syrus

You are growing bigger and stronger every day, **Baby**. With every mouthful of milk you drink, you are growing. With every breath you breathe, you are growing stronger and healthier.

A babe in a house
is a well-spring of pleasure.
Proverbial Philosophy

You deserved to be born, **Baby**. You are a unique and special design made by our Heavenly Creator. Like a rose, unlike all other roses, you are beautiful and one of a kind.

Come to the window, my baby, with me,
And look at the stars that shine on the sea!
There are two little stars that play at bo-peep
With two little fish far down in the deep;
And two little frogs cry neap, neap, neap;
I see a dear baby that should be asleep.

Nursery Rhyme

Baby, you are my dream come true! You are more beautiful than the stars that shine on the sea. You are more extraordinary than all of God's creatures.

You are beautiful in every way, **Baby**. Every part of your body is a miracle. I love each little finger and each little toe. I am in awe of how perfect you are. I love all that is you.

As wonderfully miraculous as Baby's body is, so is yours. You are beautiful in every way too, Mommy. Treat yourself in the loving and accepting way that you treat Baby.

Before I formed you in the womb I knew you;
Before you were born I sanctified you.

Jeremiah 1:5

Baby, God knows you and loves you and cares for you. You are just as precious to Him as anyone who has ever lived! You are a child of God!

This lovely and powerful affirmation is also absolutely true for you, Mommy. You, too, are as precious as anyone who has ever lived!

Clap, clap handies,
Mammy's wee, wee one;
Clap, clap handies,
Daddy's coming home.

Nursery Rhyme

Your face is beautiful and exactly you, **Baby**. Every tiny part of you is perfectly formed. I believe in you. I clap for you.

Applaud Baby often. She will learn to appreciate and applaud others as you appreciate and applaud her.

Your hands have made me
and fashioned me,
An intricate unity.
Job 10:2,8

Your little feet and legs are designed exactly right so that you can crawl and walk. Someday you will be moving around and exploring the whole world on your own, **Baby**.

Babies need the freedom to explore and do what is
spontaneous and we must nurture this freedom. At the
same time, we are responsible for their safety. As soon
as Baby begins moving around, put away anything that
can cause her harm. For the time being, pack away the
things that can be broken. Provide a safe and accepting
place for Baby to play. It isn't good for your baby to
hear "No! Don't touch." Instead provide things to touch
and say often, "Yes! Explore, touch, learn."

Surely, the smell of my son
Is like the smell of a field
Which the Lord has blessed.
Genesis 27:27

Your skin smells wonderful, **Baby**. I like to wash you and keep you clean and healthy. I like to brush your hair and care for your beautiful body. I like to hug you and cuddle you, **Baby**.

Many adults take care of themselves the way they were cared for when they were children. Keep in mind that today you are launching lifelong habits for Baby. The way you treat this little body today may be the way Baby will treat it for the rest of his life. Treat it with love today and tomorrow he will know how to treat it with kindness, too.

For you have made him
a little lower than the angels.

Psalms 8:5

I enjoy the quiet times we spend together, **Baby**.
I like to hold you while you are sleeping. I love
to watch your gentle breathing.

Set aside a special block of time for you and Baby to
spend together each day. Babies like routines and will
soon anticipate the time you will be together.

Behold, you are fair, my love!
Behold, you are fair!
You have dove's eyes.

Song of Solomon 1:15

I love to look at you, and see your sparkling eyes, **Baby**. In your eyes I see infinite possibilities for you. Your eyes are windows to eternity!

Babies enjoy looking at objects about a foot in front of them. Entertain Baby by providing mobiles and interesting objects over and near the crib. When you sit and rock together, begin showing colorful picture books. There are specially designed cloth books with large colorful pictures for babies.

I sing, I sing,
From morning 'till night,
From cares I'm free,
And my heart is light.

Nursery Rhyme

I'm glad you are a (boy/girl). You are exactly right, **Baby**. You are an angel—a gift from God. You are my sun, my moon, my star. You are my miracle, my gift from the universe.

Pat-a-cake, pat-a-cake, baker's man!
Make me a cake as fast as you can;
Pat it, and prick it, and mark it with T,
There will be enough for Baby and me.

Nursery Rhyme

You are fun to play with. I enjoy giving you care and attention, **Baby.**

Play Pat-A-Cake with Baby. Substitute for the letter "T"
the first letter of Baby's name and the whole name for
the word "Baby." You can sing the ABC song, too.
Even though the letters mean nothing to Baby today,
hearing them in a friendly way now will make them
seem like old friends later.

Baby, I really love you! It is wonderful getting to know you! We have a lot to learn from each other, and I'm enjoying every moment of our times together.

You may be surprised that Baby is developing a distinct and different personality. Is it different from what you expected? Have faith that your Loving Creator knew exactly what He was doing when He put the two of you together.

January brings the snow,
Makes our feet and fingers glow.

Nursery Rhyme

I will take you for walks in the sunshine, **Baby**. We will go many places together. I know that you like to go outside. We will share many outings.

As inviting as the sun may be to adults, sunlight is too bright for infants. Be careful when taking your baby out in the daylight. Sun bonnets and sun visors are recommended for protecting sensitive eyes. Be aware of the way things affect Baby so you can keep your little one comfortable at all times.

I cherish the special times we have together, **Baby**. I like holding you and watching you fall asleep. I enjoy the quiet times when you are sleeping and I can do the work I must do. I enjoy time with you, and I also enjoy time away from you.

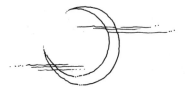

It is important to let Baby know that you like being close. It is also okay to enjoy your separate life. This affirmation will allow the child to grow as an individual rather than as an extension of you.

I treasure you more every day, **Baby**. My love for you is as big as the sun and full as the moon. I love you, **Baby**.

One way of showing love is consistency. By spending time daily with Baby, she grows to count on your being there with touches and soft words. The consistency of this will help your baby become secure with the world. It will teach her to trust others. Like the rising and the setting of the sun each day, be a constant for Baby.

Little Robin Red-breast
Sat upon a rail.
Needle, naddle, went his head,
Wiggle, waggle, went his tail.

Nursery Rhyme

———•———

Baby, each day you change, and I enjoy watching you grow. Someday you will go out into the world to discover friends and interesting things. When you go, I will always be here waiting for you to return.

When parents can distinguish between prudence and paranoia, they can give their babies the safety and freedom that they need to explore the world.
Sometimes it may be difficult to let go. Letting go is the way we teach our youngsters that the world is a safe place.

...be transformed by the renewing of your mind...
Romans 12:2

Thank you so much for coming into my life, **Baby**. You have brought many new experiences to me. I am grateful to you, because your presence is changing me into a better person. Thank you, **Baby**!

Parenting a newborn is amazing proof of the consistent building process that life is intended to be. Your baby, in all probability, will stretch you to your limits both physically and emotionally. Have faith that you will be a better, stronger, and more serene person because of the love and care you are giving to this little person.

❤ JANUARY 24

Hush-a-bye, baby, on the tree top,
When the wind blows, the cradle will rock.

Nursery Rhyme

I love gently rocking and cuddling you, **Baby**. I will calm you when you are upset or crying. I will try to always be there to comfort you when you need affection.

You can send a clear message of your love and affection for Baby by handling him in gentle ways.

Smiling girls, rosy boys,
Come and buy my little toys;
Monkeys made of gingerbread,
And sugar horses painted red.

Nursery Rhyme

You make me smile a thousand times a day. Just the thought of you, of how beautiful you are, fills my heart with joy. How glad I am that you are here, **Baby**.

Sometimes we smile inside, happy with wondrous things that happen, but we do not always let on that we are pleased. We don't let the smile shine on our faces. Try to wear your smile on the outside. It is a good gift to give Baby.

This little pig went to market;
This little pig stayed home;
This little pig had roast beef;
This little pig had none;
And this little pig cried,
'Wee, wee wee!' All the way home.

Nursery Rhyme

Your fingers and toes are beautiful. They stretch and wiggle and are perfectly formed, **Baby**. You are beautiful.

Play with Baby's toes as you recite "This Little Pig."
Make sure it doesn't tickle. Babies may laugh when
they are tickled, but that doesn't mean that they like it.
Tickling is not always fun for the receiver. Rubs and
pats are better for babies.

Keep me as the apple of your eye;
Hide me under the shadow of your wings.

Psalm 17:8

God made you to be unique and special, **Baby**.
No baby is like you. You are exactly you, and no
one else will ever be you. You are the apple of
my eye.

Did not he who made me in the womb make them?
Did not the same one fashion us in the womb?

Job 31:15

Your face is sweet and beautiful, **Baby**. When I look into your eyes I can see how much God must love and care for you.

Introduce Baby to himself by letting him see his reflection in a mirror. Some babies enjoy looking at themselves in a mirror. Does yours? There are specially designed baby toys that incorporate mirrors so Baby can see himself.

The joy I feel when I look at you fills me to the brim, **Baby**. I love you, I love you, I love you, unconditionally and forever. I will always love you with all of my heart.

><

It is good to let Baby know that she is a source of joy for you.

I treasure the sound of your voice, **Baby**. You recognize the sound of my voice. We are communicating. We will have great conversations as you grow. I will always be here to listen and talk with you.

⋘∞⋙

Try reading your favorite children's story aloud for several days in a row. Find out if Baby enjoys hearing it. If so, you have entered into a new phase of parenting–storytelling! Even tiny babies enjoy outings to the library. An early introduction to books may initiate a lifelong love for reading.

You are an important part of our family, **Baby**. You are the baby and we all love you. You are the youngest in our household, and we all hold you dear to our hearts.

A healthy family is like an orchestra. Although every-one is playing his own instrument, all are playing the same song. Teach Baby that he is part of a harmonious group.

I love all of the ways you communicate with me. It is okay to cry when you need me, **Baby**. I know that crying is the only way you can call my name.

Is Baby saying "Mama/Dada" yet? It may be the sweetest sound you will ever hear. Baby probably knows the sound of her name. Let her hear you say it many times each day.

Hush, baby, my doll, I pray you, don't cry,
And I'll give you some bread, and some milk by-and-by;
Or, perhaps, you like custard, or, maybe, a tart,
Then to either you are welcome, with all my heart.

Nursery Rhyme

I will be near when you need me, **Baby**. When you are afraid, I will listen. I will always be near to keep you safe and dry your tears.

Have you ever looked around in the darkness of Baby's room? Are scary shadows projected on the walls? Consider how things look from your child's point of view. How can you make Baby's room feel more safe and secure?

Behold, you are handsome, my beloved!
Yes, pleasant!
Song of Solomon 1:16

I love you exactly as you are, **Baby**. You are beautifully you. I wouldn't change anything about you. Some night soon I will take you outside to show you a sky full of moon.

If you honor the beauty of our planet, celebrate the moon and sun and all of God's creations, Baby will grow in appreciation of the world God has created, too.

I like to hold your little hand in my big hand. I
like to rock your tiny body in my strong arms and
take good care of you. I love you, **Baby**.

---

*It is good to remind Baby that you are separate people.
Let Baby know that he is who he is, and you are who
you are, and that you have separate and different
bodies. Enmeshed or fused relationships are unhealthy.
Since babies do not know how to let go, Mother will
have to do all of the letting go.*

Spending time with you is delightful, **Baby**. You are more important to me than cleaning my house or doing other kinds of work.

⊷══◦═══⊷

> *Mommy, be kind to yourself. Take time off just to be with Baby. The house will always need cleaning. Dusty furniture doesn't suffer emotionally if you don't spend enough time with it. Babies do.*

I will treat you with gentle love and kindness,
Baby. I will give you care and my love always.

> *Abuse can take many shapes. Telling a baby that he is
> bad can damage his self-esteem. Never shame Baby by
> saying, "You're bad," "You're not being good," "Stop
> crying," or "Shame on you!" As often as possible, make
> positive statements to Baby.*

It is okay for you to need me most of the time. I enjoy caring for you, **Baby**. You are the most important thing in my life.

Because mothering is so demanding, you must take extra care of yourself. Know that the feelings of frustration connected to the extraordinary demands of motherhood are normal feelings shared by all other mothers. Treat yourself with great love and care so that you will have the strength to care for Baby.

Rejoicing in hope, patient in tribulation,
continuing steadfastly in prayer.
Romans 12:12

Usually I will give you much patience. I will always do my best for you. If I am tired and seem short sometimes, that is part of being a human being. I won't always be tired and irritable. And no matter how I feel, I always love you, **Baby**.

It is good to tell Baby that you are not perfect.
Discussing your humanness allows the baby to grow
knowing that she doesn't have to be perfect either.

Caring for you is a pleasure. It is wonderful having you in my life, **Baby**. We will share many wonderful moments—soft, silvery pastel dawns and red pepper scarlet sunsets. I look forward to the tomorrows we will share.

Do not take to heart everything people say.
Ecclesiastes 7:21

You are exactly how you should be, **Baby**. I love everything about you, my little (prince/princess.) It is okay that you sometimes get cranky and spit up. I don't mind. All human beings are cranky sometimes.

Keep in mind that there is no perfect way to raise a child. You are the one who is the most in tune with the unique needs of Baby. You do not have to accept all of the expert advice that you read in books or hear from well-meaning relatives and friends. Let your heart guide you.

You are an incredible child. I love you, **Baby**. I enjoy seeing you suck your (thumb/fist). It is good that you can meet your own needs already and pacify yourself, **Baby**.

If Baby wants to suck more than when she is nursing or bottle- feeding, support her in that need. A pacifier may help her satisfy her strong instinct to suck. Some babies suck their thumb or fist.

Hop away, skip away, my baby wants to play;
My baby wants to play every day.

Nursery Rhyme

You are a baby. You do exactly what babies are supposed to do. You play. You eat. You are where you should be. There is no hurry to be anything or anywhere else, **Baby**.

Sometimes the world seems rushed and hurried. When talking to Baby, try to slow the pace down a bit. He is learning what the world is like through your eyes. You will teach him to be calm or frantic. Make a conscious effort to move and speak at a gentle, quiet pace.

Your hair is soft and beautiful. Your face is wonderful and sweet. You are one of the marvelous wonders of this planet. Being near you brings me great joy, **Baby**.

It is good to let Baby know that his existence brings happiness to others. It is a precious gift to his self-esteem to let him know that he can contribute to the world in a positive way by being just exactly who he is.

Roses are red,
Violets are blue.
My little Valentine,
I love you.

My precious little (girl/boy), you bring joy and laughter to my life. You are my sweetest valentine. I love you, **Baby**.

When I leave, I will always return to you, **Baby**. Sometimes I will go away from you. When I go away, I will leave you with someone whom I trust. Then I will return.

Playing peek-a-boo with Baby will help teach that you come and go, come and go, come and go. The ebb and flow of closeness and distance is healthy.

When the days begin to lengthen
The cold begins to strengthen.

Nursery Rhyme

I love you in the wintertime. This season is called winter. In the winter the weather is cold and sometimes it snows. The weather changes from hot to cold, wet to dry, bright to gloomy, but my love will never change. I love you, **Baby**.

Look out the window and see what winter looks like. Describe the things that you can see in the winter that you would not see if it were another season. If possible, bundle up Baby and go outside for a minute or two and talk about the weather. Teach Baby the sound of the word "cold."

A man's wisdom makes his face shine.

Ecclesiastes 8:1

You are very smart, **Baby**. You can cry and let me know when you are hungry, tired, or uncomfortable. You know how to express your needs even before you have learned a language. Someday we will talk about red-hot, fiery shooting stars and the big round moon.

You are as bright as sunshine, as beautiful as a flower. You are sweeter than a spring rain. I love you, **Baby**, my beautiful, beautiful (boy/girl).

When you talk to Baby, maintain eye contact. Babies like to gaze into the eyes of others. They are soothed by the voices of loved ones. Watch your baby's eyes when you are talking to him. Try always to keep in mind that Baby is studying your face and looking for clues about your emotional state. Smile at Baby often. A smile is a silent way to say, "I love you, Baby."

....aspire to lead a quiet life
I Thessalonians 4:11

You are a beautiful baby, **Baby**. You are my baby. I love to hear you laugh. I enjoy feeding you and watching you drinking milk. We don't have to be in a hurry. There is no place to go. We can sit here and be together as long as you need me.

Make each feeding calm, quiet, and leisurely. Avoid interruptions, sudden noises, bright lights, or other distractions during feeding times. Take time to gather your thoughts, snuggle Baby, and relax. Nourish yourself, Mommy, with peaceful, loving thoughts the way you are with baby. You are a good mother.

Dance, little baby, dance up high,
Never mind, baby, mother is by;
Crow and caper, caper and crow,
There, little baby, there you go;
Up to the ceiling, down to the ground,
Backwards and forwards, round and round;
Dance, little baby, and mother will sing,
With the merry carol, ding, ding, ding!

Nursery Rhyme

>─┼─◆─◦─◦─┼─◄

You may always be sure that I cherish you, **Baby**.
Many things change, but my love for you is
forever.

You can trust yourself always to love Baby. Even if in
the past, you have had relationships that did not work,
your relationship with Baby can be filled with uncondi-
tional love. Play soft music and dance slowly with Baby.
Babies usually like the swaying movement of dance.

I will treat you with true love and affection, **Baby**. You are as sweet as the perfume of roses, sweet peas, and morning glories.

Having a baby in the house may bring mixed feelings of delight, pain, and utter exhaustion. Turn to a safe person when you are worried or have questions. You do not have to do everything alone. Know that your feelings are shared by other parents. Discussing your mothering with other parents may validate your feelings and help you be more confident.

I like your many different cries. I am learning to interpret each one. It is okay to cry and be angry when you cannot tell me what you want. Until you are big enough to meet your own needs, I will try to meet all of your needs for you, **Baby**.

All humans have physical, mental, emotional, and spiritual needs. Someday Baby will learn to meet her own needs or get them satisfied with safe and supportive people. But today, you are the source of all of her satisfaction. Sometimes it may feel like a heavy burden. Rest assured as the days go by, Baby will need you less and less. Some day you will fondly look back on the exclusive relationship that you two shared.

February brings the rain,
Thaws the frozen lake again.

Nursery Rhyme

You are most precious, **Baby**. I will keep you safe. When you whimper, I will be there to comfort you. When you are hungry, I will feed you. When you are cold, I will warm you. When you are afraid, I will shelter you in my arms and keep you safe.

When traveling in your car, make sure your child is safely strapped into his car seat. Never travel without buckling up Baby.

You are exactly how you should be, **Baby**. It is okay to be an infant. You do not have to be anything else. I know you are anxious to run and play, to talk and sing—soon, Sweetheart, soon.

Listen and watch how your baby responds to you. One of the most important lessons you can teach Baby is how to communicate.

My son, hear the instruction of your father,
And do not forsake the law of your mother.

Proverbs 1:8

You can grow up to be anything you want to be,
Baby. I encourage you to grow and get bigger
every day. Someday you can be a teacher, or
dancer, or writer, or doctor. You can be and do
anything you choose. I will help you.

It is fun to think about Baby's future vocation. It is okay
to talk about Baby's future, but there is no hurry to get
there.

I love you well, my little brother,
And you are fond of me;
Let us be kind to one another,
As brothers ought to be.
You shall learn to play with me,
And learn to use my toys;
And then I think that we shall be
Two happy little boys.

Nursery Rhyme

You are perfectly you, **Baby**. Every time the sun rises strong and shiny, you become more and more special. I will always love you.

You can want what you want, **Baby**. You can be sick, angry, hungry, sleepy, and cry for my attention. I will listen. I care about your wants and needs, **Baby**.

Only you can wipe away the black cloud, gloomy and wild, that will occasionally sweep over Baby's little face. Like magic, your presence can put a shining warm smile back on her face.

I am proud of you. I cherish you, **Baby**. You
don't have to be like anyone else. You don't have
to be perfect to be lovable.

When Peter Rabbit did something he was told not to
do—go into the farmer's garden—his mother gave him
chamomile tea and put him to bed. But Peter's siblings,
Flopsy, Mopsy, and Cotton-tail, had bread and milk
and blackberries for supper. Read bits of classics to
Baby. *The Tale of Peter Rabbit* and other Beatrix Potter
works are tiny books designed especially for tiny hands.
The animal characters in each book demonstrate to children that they do not have to be perfect to be loved and
cherished.

Come, my children, come away,
For the sun shines bright today;
Little children, come with me,
Birds and brooks and posies see;
Get your hats and come away,
For it is a pleasant day.

Nursery Rhyme

I thank God for who you are, **Baby**. I pray for your health and safety every day. You are a (princess/prince), and you are important to me.

As soon as the weather permits, take Baby outside each day, even if it is only for a very short walk around the block. Your baby will get bored inside all day. Outings will stimulate all her senses.

March brings breezes loud and shrill,
Stirs the dancing daffodil.
Nursery Rhyme

You are important to me. You can trust me to make carefully considered decisions for us. You can trust my abilities to love you, **Baby**.

> *Mommy, you can trust your decision-making abilities, too. Do not be afraid to ask for help if your parenting concerns seem too great for you to handle alone. When you have trouble making a decision, sometimes deciding to ask someone for help or advice is the best decision you can make.*

MARCH 2

You will abide in my love,
just as I...abide in His love.

John 15:10

You are special to many people. Everyone loves you, **Baby**. I love you, too.

> *Name family and friends who love Baby. Tell him all*
> *about the circle of love that is all around him.*

Today we are together exactly as we are, **Baby**. You bring your feelings to us, and I bring my feelings, too. We will not always feel happy and joy-filled. Some days we may feel tired or sick. It is okay to feel exactly how you feel. All your feelings are okay, **Baby**. So are mine.

Acceptance is the great partner of love. Encourage Baby to embrace her own humanness. When you give her the space she needs for her feelings, she will grow to give others the space for their feelings.

"Thanks for noticing me."

Eeyore the Donkey

Winnie-the-Pooh by A.A. Milne

I see you, **Baby.** I notice everything about you. I see that you are more beautiful than a sky full of stars, seagulls, or sunlight. You are an extraordinary being.

Everyone likes to be noticed. When you notice Baby, even if it is nonverbal and only with your eyes or a touch, it will make him feel his importance.

Then they are glad because they are quiet.

Psalm 107:30

Every in-breath makes you stronger and stronger. With every out-breath you are growing. It is in this perfect balance of breath that you are becoming who you are meant to be. I love you, **Baby**.

Take a long deep breath, Mommy. Relax. Breathe in relaxation. Breathe out tension. Take some breathing time for yourself as you are holding Baby. As you inhale, say, "I am becoming calm." As you exhale, repeat the affirmation. Deep breathing may put some serenity back into your life. Whether you are feeling frantic or calm, your baby senses it.

Matthew, Mark, Luke, and John,
Bless the bed that I lie on.
Four corners to my bed,
Four angels over head.
Nursery Rhyme

No matter where I go, I take the thought of you with me. When we are not in the same room, I am often thinking of you. You are important to me, **Baby**.

People can exist in the minds of others. We do not have to be touching to be close. Let Baby know that even when you are not touching her, you can still be loving her with your thoughts.

When I go away from you, you may trust that I will always return. I will go. I will come back. I will go and come, go and come, but always I will return to you, **Baby**.

Never leaving Baby is not healthy. Now is the time to get a sitter to come in and care for Baby so that you can go out and rejuvenate. If you never leave Baby, he will not learn that people come and go. He may grow up feeling that leaving is abandonment. Your coming and going now will teach him that he can trust loved ones always to return to him.

Sleep, baby, sleep,
Our cottage vale is deep:
The little lamb is on the green,
With woolly fleece so soft and clean—
Sleep, baby, sleep.

Nursery Rhyme

I carry feelings of love for you wherever I go.
Sometimes when I am sleeping, **Baby**, you are
there in my dreams. Before you were born I
dreamed about having a beautiful baby like you.
You are a dream come true.

....we shall speak face to face.

III John 4

You are wonderful, and I welcome you to my life.
I have waited for you to come to me, **Baby**.
Now that you are here, we can speak face to face.

Look into Baby's eyes when you speak to her. Open communication with your face will teach her to be open, honest, and unafraid when communicating with others.

What's the news of the day,
Good neighbor, I pray?
They say the balloon
Is gone up to the moon.

Nursery Rhyme

———•———

God smiled when you were born, **Baby**. The whole planet celebrated your birth. The day you were born was (describe the day).

Let Baby know what the day of his birth was like. If you have photographs of his birth, share them with him. Describe the weather, the season, the time, the place, etc. Explain how special that day was for you and significant others. You both worked very hard that day. Discussing that process will help ease some of the struggles you have both stored subconsciously about the delivery. Highlighting the good points may help diminish the suppressed painful parts.

Blessed are the people
who know the joyful sound!
Psalm 89: 15

I like the sounds you make. I like your babbles, and coos, and your crying voice, too. I love to hear all of the sounds you make, **Baby**.

Is the sound of your voice melodic, soothing, and relaxing for your baby? Even when you are not aware of it, Baby is listening, with ears and heart, to every word you say. Remind yourself to speak in a more gentle, soothing, quiet voice today.

Everything is laughing, singing,
All the pretty flowers are springing;
See the kitten, full of fun,
Sporting in the brilliant sun;
Children too may sport and play,
For it is a pleasant day.

Nursery Rhyme

I enjoy holding, stroking, and looking at you. I love to watch you laugh, sing, and play. I love my time with you, **Baby**.

It is indeed a pleasant day, when you can hear a baby's laughter in the house. Does her laughter fill you with merriment? Your singing voice does the same for Baby.

I treasure you, **Baby**. My love doesn't depend on the way you look or behave. I love you because you are who you are. See my smiling face, and know that I love you.

Is your face as accepting to Baby's tears as his laughter? Are your eyes as accepting when he is uncooperative and fretful as when he is compliant and merry? Nonverbal messages are often more clear to Baby than words. Let your eyes as well as your lips speak of your love.

Be free to be joy-filled. Life is delightful—experience it fully. Turn your face skyward in the sunshine. When you feel happy, laugh and express that joy. I will always nurture your joy and support your enthusiasm, **Baby**.

If weather permits, take Baby for a walk today.
Celebrate our springtime planet. See the beauty
through Baby's eyes.

I will meditate on the glorious splendor....
Psalm 144:5

I enjoy touching you. I have warm feelings when I care for you. I love you, **Baby**.

When Baby senses that you genuinely care about her as a human being, she can learn to love herself and grow with a strong self-image.

Whistle, daughter, whistle; whistle, daughter dear.
I cannot whistle, mammy, I cannot whistle clear.
Whistle, daughter, whistle, whistle for a pound.
I cannot whistle, mammy, I cannot make a sound.

Nursery Rhyme

I will be close to you until you are old enough to go off on your own, **Baby**. In the meantime, I will teach you to have courage—to go forth without fear. Then someday, when it is the proper time, with love, I will let you go. But even then, and forever after, I will feel close to you. I love you my precious baby.

Whistling is like singing a wordless song. It is a cheery way to communicate. Whistle when you are working in another room to let Baby know that you are near.

You are unique, **Baby**. You are different from everyone else. I will always encourage your uniqueness.

When your child feels unconditionally accepted, you open a lifelong door that leads to a place called Trust. There he will be free to talk about his innermost secrets, fears, and concerns. In his conversations he will be real and express his true self. He will be able to give and receive genuine love.

Little Bo-Peep has lost her sheep,
And can't tell where to find them;
Leave them alone, and they'll come home,
Wagging their tails behind them.

Nursery Rhyme

I think happy thoughts of you and smile when I think of how much I love you. You are treasured, **Baby**.

Here-and-now we are touching. Here-and-now I am filled with love and joy for you, **Baby**. Here-and-now we are mother and child. That relationship is eternal. It was before. It will be after. But here-and-now is what we know best; I love our here-and-now. And I love you.

Although some people live in the past or spend their todays dreaming of the future, it is emotionally healthier to live in the present. You can begin teaching your child about making the most of the here-and-now by living in the present yourself.

Here we go up, up, up,
Here we go down, down, downy,
And here we go backwards and forwards,
And here we go round, round, roundy.

Nursery Rhyme

Sometimes the love I feel for you fills my heart so full I feel like a big balloon. I feel that I could float up to the clouds. You make me very glad to be alive. You give me purpose and bring me incredible joy, **Baby**.

Gently lift and lower Baby as you say the rhyme.
Dance around but don't be rough or jerk her little body.
Help Baby feel secure by moving her in gentle, pre-
dictable ways.

You are terrific in every way, **Baby**. You are
marvelous and a miracle. You are worthy of love.
Nothing can ever change that.

⋄⊷⊜⊶⋄

*As terrific and marvelous as Baby is, you are a basic
miracle and worthy of an abundance of love, too,
Mommy. Finding love apart from Baby is healthy.
Don't use her exclusively to meet your love needs. Find
time to be with safe, adult people who love you. It is
your responsibility to meet all of Baby's emotional
needs; it is not Baby's responsibility to meet all of yours.*

...shall flourish like a palm tree....
grow like a cedar.
Psalm 92:12

Your possibilities in life are infinite, **Baby**. I will help guide you on a life-path that will bring you to your full potential. I will study and learn so that I can help you grow in love and happiness.

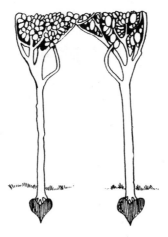

Hear my children, the instruction of a father,
And give attention to know understanding.

Proverbs 4:1

I celebrate you. I am glad that you are here,
Baby. I am glad that you are growing. I am
willing to do all that I can do to help you be
happy and fulfilled. My heart is open to each of
your needs.

"Bow-Wow," says the dog;
"Mew, mew," says the cat;
"Grunt, grunt," goes the hog;
And "squeak" goes the rat.
"Tu-whu," says the owl;
"Caw, caw," says the crow;
"Quack, quack," says the duck;
And what sparrows say you know.

Nursery Rhyme

You have a great voice, **Baby**. I like to hear you coo and gurgle. Someday you will talk, and we will have conversations. Today we can make animal sounds.

Sometimes long before babies learn to talk, they can imitate animal sounds. Make animal sounds and play animal-sound games with Baby today. Use the rhyme to get you started. Example: "Quack, quack," says the... (pause) before you say, "duck." One of the first sounds my daughter, Amy, could make was the snorting of a pig. It is such a precious memory to me.

Do not withhold good from those to whom it is due,
When it is in your power to act.

Proverbs 3:27

———

You can trust in my goodness and the strength that I bring to our relationship. I want what is good for you because I love you, **Baby**.

> *When you are not holding Baby, but he is in the room with you, send admiring glances his way. Let your body language speak to him of your great love and admiration. Whether you know it or not, Baby is often searching your face for an approving look. Your smile says, "I love you, Baby."*

Johnny's too little to whittle,
Give him some raspberry jam,
Take off his bib, put him into his crib,
And feed him on doughnuts and ham.

Nursery Rhyme

You are pretty, you are sweet; you have pretty
hands and feet. You have loving eyes, a gentle
face, silky hair, and special grace. I love you,
Baby.

Bring the hoop, and bring the ball,
Come with happy faces all;
Let us make a merry ring,
Talk and laugh, and dance and sing.
Quickly, quickly, come away,
For it is a pleasant day.

Nursery Rhyme

You are a miracle, **Baby**. Everything about your body and mind is miraculous. There are suns and moons and stars inside you—a whole universe within your soul.

You have the privilege of introducing Baby to the universe outside of himself. As soon as the weather is warm enough, take him to the park where he can see other babies and watch children at play.

It is okay that sometimes you are afraid and upset. I will not always be able to take away your upsets or hurt feelings, but I will cuddle you and give you my affection. I love you, **Baby**.

Don't invalidate a feeling that Baby may experience by saying: "Stop crying! You don't have any reason to feel angry, sad, or mad." If you tell her that she shouldn't feel the way she is feeling, she will begin to question her feelings and doubt herself. Validate all of her feelings by acknowledging them as part of being human. Sometimes just expressing the feeling and sharing it will lessen the impact for her. You may choose to say something like: "I know how you feel. Sometimes I feel that way too. All humans feel sad sometimes. But your sadness will not last forever. Soon you will feel happy again."

It takes a great deal of courage to grow and
become a child. You are courageous and growing
every day. I am proud of you, **Baby**.

*What we are within is mirrored outside of us. Your
baby will read your face as carefully as he listens to your
words. Smile and look at Baby when you talk to him.
If you are feeling angry, depressed, or anxious, it will
show on your face. You may want to tell your baby
how you are feeling and that it isn't because of him that
you are feeling that way. Speak honestly about your
feelings even when you do not think Baby is old enough
to understand.*

❤ MARCH 30

March winds and April showers
Bring forth May flowers.
Nursery Rhyme

You are filled with goodness. Your goodness will grow as you grow. I am proud of you, **Baby**. You are soft and warm and cuddly, **Baby**. My heart sings when I look at you.

Like rains and winds that clean the air and earth, tears and tantrums will wash away Baby's tensions. Don't feel that you have to stop her from crying the instant that she starts. Since Baby cannot walk and run and let out energy, sometimes crying is her only way of releasing tension.

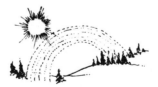

Trip and go, heave and ho!
Up and down, to and fro;
From the town to the grove,
Two and two, let us rove,
Nursery Rhyme

Your body is changing every day. You are growing bigger and stronger, **Baby**. Your hair is growing longer; your feet and hands are getting bigger. I enjoy watching you learn how to do wonderful things with your body.

Name things Baby can do: roll over, sit up, crawl, etc.
Tell him how proud you are that he can do these things.
Applaud all of his accomplishments.

April brings the primrose sweet,
Scatters daisies at our feet.

Nursery Rhyme

❦

We will celebrate our beautiful planet together,
Baby. The world has many extraordinary sights
to see. I will take you to parks and farms and
beaches and zoos and big cities. We will go to
many places, you and I.

If weather permits, take Baby outside in a stroller or a
carriage for a short walk today. Point out the beautiful
things around him. Describe the color of the sky, grass,
flowers, clouds, and animals. Someday you will walk
hand in hand with your child through primrose and
daisies in search of little spotted bugs. There is so much
to look forward to, Mommy!

Even the sparrow has found a home,
And the swallow a nest for herself.
Where she may lay her young.

Psalms 84:3

I will hold you and give you the love you need to grow, **Baby**. You do not have to struggle to survive. I will care for you. I will give you food and a resting place. I am here for you. I love you, **Baby**.

Be still, and know that I am God.

Psalms 46:10

God lives within you, **Baby**. His goodness is part of your being. As you grow, I will help you learn to be still so you can hear the small still voice within that will guide you along your life-path. Everything is unfolding exactly as it should unfold.

You are a miracle, **Baby**. I will take time to celebrate the miracle and thank God for the
opportunity to be with you. Being with you
Baby, enriches my life.

*Teaching your child about the power of prayer and faith
in God will be a gift that will carry her through difficult
times for all of her lifetime. Letting Baby know that you
thank God for the opportunity you have of being her
mother will open the door for a life of thanksgiving.*

The shadow cast by the rose's thorny branches
Shades the rich, moist soil the buds need to open and bloom.

I will keep you safe, **Baby**. I will protect you from harm and provide for your needs. I am big, and I will watch over you daily. I will help you bloom into the beautiful person that you are.

> *Mommy, you are the rich, moist soil in which your "rose" is growing. Your arms are the branches that support him. Your love is the sunshine that nourishes his spirit. Your words of encouragement are the dew drops that give him life.*

Little maid, little maid,
Whither goest thou?
Down in the meadow
To milk my cow.
Nursery Rhyme

Today I will be especially gentle with you, **Baby**. I will hold you in silence and thank God for the miraculous creature that you are, and for the opportunity I have been given to share in your growth.

To everything there is a season,
A time for every purpose under heaven:
A time to be born, and a time to die;
A time to weep, and a time to laugh.

Ecclesiastes 3: 1, 2, 4

It is okay that you cry. I know it is your way of telling me when you are hungry or uncomfortable. Tears wash away anger and pain, **Baby**. You may cry when you feel like crying.

Crying helps Baby shut out bright lights, loud sounds, other uncomfortable sensations, and allows her to release tension. When Baby chooses to cry, grant her that freedom. Don't take the crying personally. Hold her and sing softly and allow the tears to flow.

Every one of your feelings is okay, **Baby**. It is okay that sometimes you are fussy. Sometimes I feel cranky and tired, too. I will help you learn ways of expressing all of your feelings.

Sometimes babies are fussy because of the discomfort caused by trapped gas bubbles. The discomfort is often relieved by burping the baby. Have you burped your baby today?

Every part of your body is wonderful, **Baby**.
Your little ears are learning to listen and hear the
sounds around you. Hear my voice telling you
how extraordinary you are.

*Most babies like soft music. Play gentle music for Baby,
and see if it soothes him to sleep. He may also like to
listen to you singing a lullaby or reading a story.
Repeatedly singing the same song or reading the same
story to Baby will help him gain a sense of security.*

A sunshiny shower
Won't last half an hour.
Nursery Rhyme

❧•❦

When I see your face, **Baby**, I am filled with joy.
Your smile warms me like sunlight.

Now is a time of opportunity. Be open and ready to
find guidance that you need to be happy with Baby.
Take pleasure in simple things: herb tea, a warm bath, a
bouquet of spring blossoms, your baby's smiling face,
and other things that you especially like. Treat yourself
with love, Mommy.

Like a lily among thorns,
So is my love....

Song of Solomon 2:2

❖

I give you unconditional love. You don't have to do anything to earn my love—it is a gift. I will always give my love to you, **Baby**. Even when I am no longer on this earth, I will love you from the Hereafter. I will be your mother for eternity.

How many miles is it to Babylon?
Threescore miles and ten.
Can I get there by candle-light?
Yes, and back again!
If your heels are nimble and light,
You may get there by candle-light.

Nursery Rhyme

I share in your delight of discovering the world. As your eyes discover colors and shapes and beauty, you are discovering the exciting world, **Baby**.

Watching Baby, you will see things with enormous satisfaction. You will see the world in new and extraordinary ways.

Your work is to play. Play with your toys. Play with me. Play with others. I like to watch you play, **Baby**.

———⊷∙⊷———

In order to be emotionally healthy, Baby needs lots of spontaneous play. Play is the natural instinct most often suppressed in troubled families. Having fun with Baby is the best way to teach her how to play.

"I bring you good tidings of great joy...."
Luke 2:10

I experience new heights of joy, love, and pride when I am with you. You give me many gifts, **Baby**.

It is good for Baby to know that he is contributing to your happiness. Even infants can feel a sense of worth. Your baby will feel valuable when he knows he is a source of joy for you.

Praise him, sun and moon:
Praise him, all you stars of light.

Psalms 148:3

Every day you grow more alert and responsive. That is very good, **Baby**. I can tell that you are listening when I talk to you. You talk to me with your bright eyes.

Have you noticed that Baby is beginning to move her body more smoothly and with greater coordination? As the sun and moon appear and reappear, Baby is growing–changing. Her season of growth is now. You are the fertile soil in which the roots are planted and from which her whole being stretches skyward.

Our Creator has given you a miraculous and wonderful body. You are growing. Someday you will be a grown-up person, **Baby**. We are close, but at the same time, we are separate bodies.

Healthy relationships are open and flexible and allow fulfillment of both people. For Baby's emotional growth, you must encourage his separateness. Acknowledge him every time he takes a developmental step. Celebrate each milestone: raising head and chest, grasping, smiling, saying first word, getting to a sitting position, crawling, creeping on hands, pulling himself to a standing position, and taking first steps away from you.

The Lord shall preserve your going out and your coming in
From this time forth, and even forevermore.

Psalms 121:8

Today as I hold you, **Baby**, I realize how quickly you are growing. Every day you are different and a bit older. I celebrate you here and now, as you are today. I cherish every moment we share.

I love you in this season called spring, **Baby**.
Spring is a wonderful time to be alive. In the
spring baby animals are born and flowers bloom.

---

*Today take Baby for a walk and look for signs of spring.
On your walk, describe how in the springtime plants
bud, flowers bloom, and baby animals are born.
Explain how all animals have a mother and that
mammals give their young milk. Describe things on the
walk that are happening because it is springtime. It
doesn't matter that Baby may not understand your
explanations; the words will enrich her world.*

Time runs a quick race.

Proverb

———•+•———

It is my pleasure to take good care of you, **Baby**. It is okay that you get dirty and messy. When I was a baby, (name your care givers) took care of me. Someday you may take care of others.

Some days it may seem that you will always be caring for this tiny person, but remember, time runs a quick race. Enjoy this day that you have together. Baby will never be exactly this age again. It is God's perfect design that we should do for each other. Take a few minutes today to think about how it might have been for your mother (care giver) taking care of you when you were an infant. Send a silent message of love and gratitude to her.

I will care for you with all of the love that I bring to our togetherness. I accept the heavy responsibility of teaching you about relating to others. I love you, **Baby**.

Some psychologists believe that the model for each person's intimate relationships begins with his first care giver. The modeling that takes place during Baby's infancy will establish lifelong patterns. When Baby gets older and is dealing with others, he may expect them to respond to him in the same way you responded to him as an infant. Happy, kind, orderly care-giving will give him a sense of well-being today and establish a standard for loving and kind relationships with healthy people tomorrow. Angry, depressed, chaotic handling can make him insecure now and make intimate relationships difficult or impossible for him later.

You are smart. You have been created with a great mind. You think and learn and find out about the world with your brain. You have extraordinary intelligence, **Baby**.

Our thoughts produce our reality. When we have happy thoughts, we make the world around us positive. You can teach Baby about being positive by surrounding her with love and affection and uplifting affirmations every time you interact with her. The emotional climate experienced today will establish lifelong standards for her.

Bye, baby bunting,
Daddy's gone hunting,
Gone to get a rabbit skin
To wrap the baby bunting in.
Nursery Rhyme

I know that it takes patience to wait to be diapered and dressed. I know that you would like to wiggle around and play. As you get older, sitting still for a short time will not be so difficult. I will show my love for you by being patient. I love you, **Baby**.

The only way Baby will learn patience is to observe others being patient. Today strive to have patience with Baby's impatience.

Soon you will be able to say many things. You are making more and more sounds each day. It is exciting to know that you are trying to talk to me, **Baby**.

To help Baby increase his understanding of words, talk to him as much as possible. Your conversations will glean new significance as his vocabulary grows.

You are getting big, **Baby**. It is fun for you to move around on your own. Moving from place to place is a good sign that you are growing.

When Baby begins to move around on her own, it is exhilarating for her. At the same time, this new mobility creates a need for extra caution. Be careful around pools of water. Never leave her unattended in high places. Don't smoke, eat, drink, or carry hot objects while holding Baby. When you are with Baby, just relax and enjoy. The many things that you need to do will still be there when your time with Baby has ended.

God bless the master of this house,
The mistress bless also,
And all the little children
That round the table go.

Nursery Rhyme

This is your house. It is a good and safe place for you. I know that sometimes it gets noisy. I will try to buffer the sounds of the world for you because I love you, **Baby**.

Most babies are afraid of loud noises. Don't yell at or around Baby. Bless your child with calm, quiet speech and gentle, kind touches.

Love one another; as I have loved you.

John 13:34

I love you every day, **Baby**. Some days I don't know exactly what you need from me. Some days you may not even know what you need yourself. But I will listen and try to meet your needs.

There will be times when Baby's needs all seem to be met, and yet he cries. Vary your responses to include: singing, walking, talking, rocking, playing. If he is teething, there are special pacifiers that can be chilled in the refrigerator (not frozen in freezer) that will help cool his gums. Rubbing his gums gently with one finger may be soothing, too.

In April's sweet month,
When the leaves begin to spring
Little lambs skip like fairies
And birds build and sing.

Nursery Rhyme

Someday you will come to understand all of my words. Then you will know that I love you unconditionally, **Baby**.

One, two, buckle my shoe;
Three, four, shut the door;
Five, six, pick up sticks;
Seven, eight, lay them straight;
Nine, ten, a good fat hen.

Nursery Rhymes

Soon you will be able to do things for yourself, **Baby**. I know that not being able to care for yourself or communicate your needs can be both boring and frustrating. Someday you will be able to dress yourself, put on your shoes, and go outside to play—all by yourself!

As Baby grows, she will learn to entertain herself for longer periods of time. Her constant need for you will diminish each day. Today, try to help her feel less bored and frustrated about her total dependency upon others by reassuring her of her continuing growth.

Pease-porridge hot, pease-porridge cold,
Pease-porridge in the pot, nine days old.
Nursery Rhyme

❀❀

I know that you like your feeding time, **Baby**. I enjoy this time with you, too. I love watching you eat. You are growing bigger every day.

Do you know that pease-porridge is pea soup? If Baby is eating baby food, the nursery rhyme is a good one to say when you feed him peas. You can teach him things like hot and cold, and different flavors by naming them as he is experiencing each one.

Daffy-Down-Dilly has come up to town,
In a fine petticoat and a green gown.

Nursery Rhyme

You look very pretty today, **Baby**. Do you like the clothes that you are wearing? Do you like the colors? Touch your clothes. How do they feel? Someday you will choose your own clothes and dress yourself.

Does Baby seem to prefer certain outfits more than others? Does she have a favorite color? Watch her eyes when you dress her. Feel the material and make sure it is soft and comfortable for Baby. You can introduce the color words to Baby by naming them as you are dressing her.

May brings flocks of pretty lambs,
Skipping by their fleecy dams.

Nursery Rhyme

Many people love you, **Baby**. Our family—you
and I and (name the people who live in your
house)—all love you. We have friends who love
you, too.

> *It is important to let Baby know that he is loved by*
> *people besides you. Name the members of the family*
> *and friends of the family. Sing songs about all of the*
> *people Baby knows. Show Baby their photographs.*
> *This will help establish strong bonding with extended*
> *family members.*

❤ May 2

I will help you be your real self. Life can be a
wonderful adventure. I will help you live your
life to the fullest, **Baby**.

In the book, _The Velveteen Rabbit_, when the nursery
magic Fairy told the Velveteen Rabbit that she turned
the old and worn-out toys into Real, the rabbit asked,
"Wasn't I Real before?" The fairy assured him that he
had been real to the little boy because the boy loved
him. Read to Baby portions of _The Velveteen Rabbit_ by
Margery Williams. You may choose to buy her a velveteen rabbit this spring. Most babies enjoy touching
soft materials like velvet and satin.

A fine song I have made
To please you, my dear;
And if it's well sung,
It will be charming to hear.
Nursery Rhyme

I will sing a song for you that encourages you to smile. If my song puts a smile on your face, I am happy, for then I will know you are happy, **Baby**. Someday you will sing for me, and I will smile and listen to your sweet song.

*How beautiful upon the mountains
Are the feet of him who brings good news,
Who proclaims peace,
Who brings glad tidings of good things.*

Isaiah 52:7

You have good muscles and strong bones, **Baby**. You flex and straighten your little legs. You will be able to crawl and walk and run someday. Your feet will carry you to many interesting places. Do you want to go on a pretend bike ride today?

Some babies like to have help exercising their legs and arms. Place Baby on his back and put his feet in your hands. Gently move his legs back and forth as if he is riding a bicycle. Move his little arms in the same gentle way. Does he enjoy the exercising? If he does, take him "bicycling" often—especially on days when he seems to be irritable.

You are getting bigger every day, **Baby**.
Someday you will be a grown-up. You have my
permission to be as big as I. You have my permission to be smaller than I. You have my
permission to be bigger than I. Any size that you
are is perfect for you.

▸┤◂▸┄○┄◂┤◂

*Each month most babies gain approximately one and
one-half to two pounds and grow one to one and one-
half inches. Usually heads grow faster than the rest of
the body, so don't worry if Baby's head seems out of
proportion. This is quite normal; Baby's body will soon
catch up with the size of the head.*

Now is the time to be happy, **Baby**. Now is the time to play. Now is the time to be joy-filled and to enjoy all that is around you.

You have every hope for Baby to be a happy person. Choosing to be happy or choosing not to be happy is a decision that people make about their lives. You can teach Baby to choose happiness by your positive attitude about life.

Dance, Thumbkin, dance.
Dance, Pointer, dance.
Dance, Longman, dance.
Dance, Ringman, dance.
Dance, Pinky, dance.
Dance, ye merry men, dance.
Nursery Rhyme

You are a baby today. You won't be a baby very long. I will celebrate each of your baby days. I will cherish you as you grow, **Baby**.

Use your fingers to sing the nursery rhyme to baby. To make the fingers dance, wiggle appropriate finger when reciting each line. You can play a guessing game by singing the rhyme and hiding your hands behind your back. Example: Where is Thumbkin? Where is Thumbkin? (Hands behind back) Here he is, here he is! (Wiggle appropriate fingers where Baby can see them.)

I love you, **Baby**. I love others, too. I especially love (name people you love). I like spending time with you; I enjoy spending time with others, too.

Does it seem nearly impossible to find time to be with your friends and family? You may have less energy to go out because of the baby's constant demands. Don't become imprisoned by motherhood; make time to go out without the baby. Enjoy yourself. When you return, you will be a better, rested mother.

It is okay to cry, **Baby**. Sometimes when you are alone in your crib and you feel sad, you cry for me, and I come and give you hugs. When I cuddle you, I know it makes you feel good. I like making you feel good. Making you feel good makes me feel good, **Baby**.

*Every good gift and every perfect gift is from above,
and comes down from the Father of lights.*

James 1:17

You are God's perfect gift to me. I will try to be there whenever you call me, **Baby**. I know you need me, even in the middle of the night.

Mommy, do you sometimes experience sudden crying episodes or feelings of mild depression? Are you exhausted because you must wake up many times each night to feed Baby? Have you tried:

napping during the day?

taking time out each day to be alone?

asking someone to help you with Baby at night?

making an effort not to get overly tired during the day?

sharing your feelings with another parent?

Be really whole
And all things will come to you.

Lao Tsu

꧁꧂

Look at you, **Baby**. Your whole body is wonderful. Look at your little toes. Aren't they cute? Let's count them. (Count them.) Look at your little fingers. Aren't they beautiful? Let's count them. (Count each one.) All your parts are extraordinary. My memories of you will always live within me. My love for you will never end.

I always love you, **Baby**. I will usually come to you when you cry. I may not always come immediately. If I do not come at the exact moment you first call to me, it doesn't mean that I have stopped loving you. It means that I am busy and I cannot come right then.

It is best to go to Baby when she cries because it establishes a sense of her importance and teaches her that she has some power in this world. As she gets older, you may not respond as quickly as you did at first. Gradually allowing small amounts of time where Baby must wait to have her needs met will help her learn patience.

You are terrific in every way, **Baby**. I like you exactly the way you are. I wouldn't change anything about you. I have memorized every tiny detail of your miraculous body. I can close my eyes and see you as clearly as if my eyes were open.

In a personal way, describe to Baby all of the ways his body is wonderful. Use words that describe his uniqueness to show him how special he is. Example: Your hair is curly and blond, your skin is soft and black, your nose has freckles, your chin has a dimple. If you affirm the wonder of his body, he will learn self-worth.

It is okay that you need me to meet all of your physical needs, **Baby**. I will try to meet your emotional needs as well. You can depend on me to help you be healthy and strong.

❦

From the second we are born we have needs. Every one of Baby's needs is healthy and normal. In a functional family, Baby will have her needs met in healthy ways. You may not be able to meet all of her needs alone. Don't hesitate asking for help when you need it. Father, siblings, and extended family members often welcome the opportunity to contribute to Baby's well-being. Letting others do for Baby makes them feel important, it gives you time to rest, and it meets Baby's needs. Everyone wins!

You don't have to hurry, **Baby**. It takes lots of days to grow. We will enjoy your growing season together. "Slow and steady wins the race."

In Aesop's fable, The Tortoise and the Hare, the tortoise beat the rabbit in a race. Although the rabbit was quicker, the tortoise had tenacity. When parenting, remember Tortoise's motto: "Slow and steady wins the race."

"Yaup, yaup, yaup!"
Said the croaking voice of a frog:
"A rainy day
In the month of May,
And plenty of room in the bog."
Nursery Rhyme

✦━◉ ◉━✦

Baby, I love you. I love you. I love you, I do. I love all that you are now and all that you will be tomorrow.

People spend their spare time doing what they love to do best. When you spend time with Baby, he knows that he is important and that you love to be with him. Giving time is a monumental demonstration of your love. Today read a book or sing a song. Play a game or take a walk.

Cross Patch,
Draw the latch,
Sit by the fire and spin;
Take a cup,
And drink it up,
And call your neighbors in.

Nursery Rhyme

Holding you in my lap—wrapping my arms around you—gives me an overwhelming feeling of joy. I will keep you safe in my arms, **Baby**.

As you generously give Baby the safety of yourself, who will shelter and nurture you, Mommy? Today take time to daydream, focus on your inner feelings, or share a cup of tea with a friend. Nurture the baby within yourself. To be the best mother that you can be, seize every opportunity that you get to rejuvenate and enjoy yourself.

You are wonderful and special. You don't have to be perfect, **Baby**. Human beings are never perfect. Being human is what makes us unique and lovable.

As important as it is for Baby to learn that being perfect is impossible, it is just as important for you to internalize that you don't have to be "the perfect parent." Do the very best that you can, and trust in the knowledge that as Baby is growing, you are growing in your ability to parent. Read and study, or talk to someone when you have parenting questions.

You are beautifully unique. I am very proud of you, **Baby**. You are a special creature of the universe. You are so very special to me.

Don't be too hard on yourself in the beginning if you secretly make comparisons between Baby and your other children or other people's babies. Don't feel guilty if you think that Baby is not as alert or as beautiful as another baby. This is a natural feeling; other mothers have the same concerns about their babies, too. As Baby's own personal qualities emerge, you will be proud of her unique beauty.

There were two blackbirds
Sitting on a hill.
The one named Jack,
And the other named Jill.
Fly away, Jack!
Fly away, Jill!
Come again, Jack!
Come again, Jill!
Nursery Rhyme

I am glad that you are part of our family, **Baby**. We love you.

Families come in all sizes. It may be just you and Baby; your family might include a dozen, or some number in between. No matter what the size, don't be over-whelmed by sibling rivalry. Time and patience will help you adjust and learn to be a family. Just like people, families do not have to be perfect. Being a family is an ongoing process. The home is a place to practice rela-tionships, a place to learn how to get along.

Behold, children are an heritage from the Lord:
The fruit of the womb is a reward.
Psalms 127:3

❯•❮

You are a gift from God, **Baby.** You will only be a baby for a short time. I will honor each day that we have together and make it count for us.

Children do not belong to us. God loans them to us for a short time. It is our responsibility to nurture them and help them grow. We must do the best we can to meet their physical and emotional needs during their season of growing.

Sing song! Merry go round,
Here we go up to the moon, Oh!
Little Johnnie a penny has found,
And so we'll sing a tune, Oh!

Nursery Rhyme

I see your eyes dancing when you are happy. It is good to be happy and to sing a merry song. I love you, **Baby**.

Most likely Baby's favorite musical instrument is still the sound of your voice. You can give him the gift of other beautiful sounds. Softly play different kinds of music for him. Watch his reactions. Does he like certain kinds of music better than others? Use soft music both to soothe and to stimulate Baby.

I will shelter you in my arms and always keep you safe, **Baby**. When I hold you in my arms, and watch your eyes begin to close, and see you dozing, I feel very protective of you.

Do not disown or neglect your own needs, Mommy. You are the most important person for meeting Baby's needs. Who will shelter and protect you? To flourish, you must see yourself as a basic miracle and worthy of love, too. Surround yourself with a support system of safe, helpful people.

I am thankful to share a place in time with you. For the next twenty years or more, we will share a space. I accept the responsibility of caring for you, **Baby**. I welcome the opportunity to support you in all the ways I can.

———◆———

Have feelings of love and commitment surfaced that you worried might never happen? Have other feelings of anxiety associated with the tremendous responsibility of caring for Baby been unleashed? Most parents wrestle with these conflicting emotions. Know that all of the feelings of parenting that you are experiencing, negative as well as positive, are okay.

Polly, put the kettle on,
Polly, put the kettle on,
Polly, put the kettle on,
We'll all have tea.

Nursery Rhyme

Let's have a party, **Baby**, just you and me. Today we can have our first tea party. We will have lots of other tea parties while you are growing. We can have a tea party anytime you want to have a quiet moment with me.

A tea party doesn't have to mean drinking tea. Warm milk and zwieback might be the treats for your first tea party with Baby. Seize every opportunity to celebrate the day. My Sarah loved tea parties when she was a little girl. The ritual of quiet parties with her as she was growing weaved wonderful memories in the fabric of those days we shared.

Jesus called them to Him and said,
"Let the little children come to me,
and do not forbid them;
for of such is the kingdom of God."
Luke 18:16

Your open eyes are bright. Your face and body are quiet. I enjoy watching your alertness, **Baby**. I know that you hear my words. Trust that what I tell you is the truth.

If you know these things,
blessed are you if you do them.
John 13:17

I treasure the moments when we can sit quietly
together. You don't have to do anything. I like
you just the way you are, **Baby**. I am in no
hurry to leave you. I will take this time to be still
and listen for the voice within.

Assuredly, I say to you,
whoever does not receive the kingdom of God
as a little child will by no means enter it.
Luke 18:17

You and I are close today. My heart beats near your heartbeat. I cherish the closeness that we share, **Baby**. I treasure the nearness of you, and the uniqueness of you.

You, therefore, who teach another,
do you not teach yourself?

Romans 2:21

More and more I learn each day as I peer into your eyes. Watching you is teaching me about all human beings and the universe. You are my teacher, and I am yours, **Baby**.

I watch you growing every day, **Baby**. I notice all of the ways in which you are changing. I celebrate every aspect of your uniqueness.

Discover all the positive and beautiful things in Baby. List them. Share the wonderful list with others in the presence of Baby. Let Baby hear you complimenting him before others.

I care about you and all of your needs. I want us to be close, **Baby**.

Display your love for Baby. Maintain a climate of caring. Happy infants bond more easily with their mother than do sad ones. To cement this important bond, provide a loving, gentle environment for Baby.

June brings tulips, lilies, roses,
Fills the children's hands with posies.

Nursery Rhyme

Baby, I love you unconditionally. I will always love you. You do not have to do anything to earn my love. It is a gift. I do not love you because of anything that you do. I love you because you are God's little child. He has given you to me. And He loves us both—unconditionally.

I love you, **Baby**. I cannot always be with you, but I love you even when we are not together.

Tell Baby when you are going to leave the room. Tell her where you are going and when you will be back. For example: "I am going out of the room now, Baby. I will be back soon. You will be okay alone. I will be in the next room. If you need me, you can cry out, and I will come back." You can reassure her with the sound of your voice from another room and help her feel safe when you leave her alone for short periods of time.

I love to see your smiling face, **Baby**. Your sweet smile warms my heart and my whole being. Your smile is a gift you give to others.

When you talk sincerely and interestingly with Baby, you are promoting his feeling of self-worth. Don't limit your speaking vocabulary when talking to him. Converse with him the way you would with grown-ups. The vocabulary he hears today is the language he will command tomorrow.

Yankee Doodle went to town
Upon a little pony;
He stuck a feather in his hat,
And called it Macaroni.

Nursery Rhyme

✦━◗◖━✦

You change every day. I enjoy watching the changes in you. I like everything about you, **Baby**. I liked who you were yesterday, who you are today, and who you will be tomorrow.

As Baby grows, you will begin to understand her general temperament and become more self-confident in your mothering. You are changing daily, too. Have you ever thought that as much as you enjoy watching Baby, she enjoys watching you that much, too? It is a mirror of admiration. Baby thinks you are the most beautiful person in the world. Truly.

Wash me, and comb me,
And lay me down softly,
And set me on a bank to dry;
That I may look pretty
When someone comes by.

Nursery Rhyme

You are a pleasure to look upon. Your head feels like a sweet peach. I like your cute little body. I love your (soft/chubby) legs and arms. Your back is straight. Your neck is good and strong and holds up your beautiful head. Every tiny detail of your body is unique and special. I love you, **Baby**.

You have the right to move away from me,
Baby. You may leave and I know that you will
return. We can come and go from each other.
Every afternoon the sun goes down but every
morning it returns to light the new day just as we
return to each other.

*When Baby begins to crawl or move away from you,
reassure him with cheerful words. Encourage him with
smiles of pride as he takes healthy steps away from you.
Let him know that he can count on you as a secure base
from which to venture.*

Wash the dishes, wipe the dishes,
Ring the bell for tea;
Three good wishes, three good kisses,
I will give to thee.

Nursery Rhyme

I know that your needs change quickly, **Baby**. I will gently rub and soothe away your tired, tense, crabby moments. Don't fret, my darling. You soon will feel better.

Be perceptive of Baby's emotional shifts. Acknowledge them as okay feelings. Help her feel better with gentle touches and softly spoken words of encouragement, and don't take her crying personally.

A light to those who are in darkness....
a teacher of babes....
Romans 2:19, 20

❖•❖

You are learning new things every day. I will help you learn to do for yourself; you can trust me to teach you, **Baby**. You can trust you to learn. We are partners in your education.

> *Your love and caresses enable Baby to cope with the world. Providing loving attention and support will help Baby grow with the knowledge that he can trust himself, he can trust you, and he can trust the rest of the world, too.*

Monday's child is fair of face,
Tuesday's child is full of grace,
Wednesday's child is full of woe,
Thursday's child has far to go,
Friday's child is loving and giving,
Saturday's child has to work for a living.
But a child that's born on the Sabbath day
Is fair and wise and good and gay.

Nursery Rhyme

You can always return to me for a hug, a pat, a cuddle, or a kiss. I will be there when you need love. You can "ask" for affection when you need it, and I will give it to you. I love you, **Baby**.

Be Baby's beacon of security. Teach her to ask for affection when she needs it so that as she grows, she will not have to act in negative ways to get your attention. Teach her that she can ask to have her needs met—what an incredible gift to give your child!

Friday night's dream, on Saturday told,
Is sure to come true, be it never so old.

Nursery Rhyme

It feels so good to know that you are near me,
and we will share time today. I look forward to
touching your face and seeing you smile. I am
glad for today. You are a dream come true,
Baby.

I like to keep you dry. When I was a baby, someone kept me dry. Someday you may care for your baby. Human beings take turns caring for each other. I like to take care of you because I love you, **Baby**.

Use diapering time to enhance Baby's sense of pride for his body. Your attitude towards diapering will convey a very strong message to Baby. Teach him that body functions are a positive rather than a negative part of life.

Be kindly affectioned to one another with brotherly love,
in honor giving preference to one another.

Romans 12:10

I honor you with gentle rubs. Sharing touches is an essential part of love. Your body is beautiful, **Baby**. I will teach you how to care for it.

> *Massage Baby's back. It will help her relax and give her great pleasure. Gentle strokes and affection are ways of honoring another. Treat Baby with love, and she will learn to give love.*

I promise I love you, **Baby**.

> *Sometimes when you hold Baby, you may see his little*
> *chin quiver or his hands tremble in fear. Expressing*
> *your love will help him feel more secure and less afraid.*

I am here to feed you today, as I was here to feed you yesterday, and the day before, and the day before that. You can count on me, **Baby**, to be here to feed you when you are hungry.

When Baby learns to trust that you will meet her physical needs, she can then begin to grow with a sense of self-worth. Responsible, gentle care-giving sends Baby a clear message of your love.

I love you more each new day, **Baby**. The sun comes up over there (point to the east) in the morning. The sun goes down over there (point to the west) in the afternoon. The stars twinkle and light the sky every night. When it is light, most people work and play or nap. When it is dark, usually people sleep. Day and night happen over and over and never end, just as my love for you will never end.

———

Everyday experiences and predictable routines are reassuring to infants. Baby will enjoy knowing what to expect. Routines will give him a sense of security. Describe the routines of our universe, such as dawn and dusk, to Baby.

There's a neat little clock,
In the schoolroom it stands,
And it points to the time
With its two little hands.

Nursery Rhyme

———•———

Today I will take time to play with you. I will give you the gift of my time. I love you, **Baby**.

Play is a crucial part of Baby's development. Be open and supportive of all of the games she chooses to play. Don't wait until tomorrow to play. Do it today. We cannot get back the time that is lost. We cannot make up for undone things. Baby will only learn to play and enjoy life if you show her, by your example, how it is done.

Is anyone cheerful?
Let him sing psalms.
James 5:13

I am a good, loving mother. I am your mother. I offer you the security of my lap. My arms will provide a safe place where you can rest, **Baby**. You are welcome always to come to me, and I will wrap myself around you and sing you a lullaby. Even when you are a grown-up and perhaps bigger than I am, I will still love you, **Baby**.

I love my love with an A,
because he's Agreeable.

Nursery Rhyme

I love you in so many ways; I cannot even count them all. I love you in more ways than there are stars in the sky, **Baby**.

Think of some of the ways you love Baby and use all of the letters of the alphabet to make up a rhyme just for him. Example: I love my Eric with an E, because he's energetic. One of my favorite memories of my son, Eric's early years was how he liked to go outside at night and count the stars. He really thought he could count them all!

The Man in the Moon looked out of the moon,
Looked out of the moon and said,
"It's time for all children on the earth
To think about getting to bed!"
Nursery Rhyme

You are beautiful, especially in your sleeping. Go to sleep, my little sleepyhead. Take your nap. When you awaken, I will be here to give you my attention, **Baby**.

Mommy, do you sometimes experience strong mood swings? It's okay and normal after giving birth to have some depressing days. Some of it is due to changes in the amount of hormones in your body and the exhaustion of caring for Baby. Just remember that these emotions are normal and they will not last forever. Taking a nap when Baby naps may give you the extra energy boost you need.

Little drops of water,
Little grains of sand,
Make the mighty ocean,
And the pleasant land.
Nursery Rhyme

I love and value you, **Baby**. One thing I love
best about you is, (state specific example).
Another thing I love about you is (state another
specific example). Some things that make you
unique and special are (state more specific examples).

Give Baby new, soothing auditory imprints each day.
Compose personal compliments suitable for your
unique baby. Instill a positive, reassuring inner voice
that Baby will unconsciously hear for the rest of her life.
Someday the words you speak today, like little drops of
water or little grains of sand, will become as big as the
mighty ocean and the pleasant land.

I am glad that you are my baby. We celebrate the here-and-now. You tether me to the present. I love our togetherness, **Baby**.

Infancy is an unique time when we are totally grounded in the present. Unlike adults, children are always in the here-and-now. See the world through Baby's eyes, and be grounded in the joy of the moment.

Oh, give thanks to the Lord, for he is good!
For his love endures forever.

Psalm 118:1

❋❋

I will do my best to nourish your body and your spirit. I know that my holding you and telling you how much I love you is as nurturing to your spirit as milk is to your body. I love you, **Baby**.

Infants must be touched and stimulated in order to grow physically. Studies have proven that children who are denied being held and stroked often become sick or even die. Touches need to accompany the positive verbal encouragement so that Baby can grow emotionally strong.

Here's Sulky Sue,
What shall we do?
Turn her face to the wall
Till she comes to.

Nursery Rhyme

Baby, it is okay to feel exactly how you are feeling. Your feelings are never wrong. Feelings are just feelings. Like the rain, sad feelings will not last very long. Like sunshine, good feelings will soon return to warm you.

It is never too early to begin helping Baby identify and acknowledge his feelings. When you discuss feelings, you are giving your child the vocabulary he will later need to express and handle his emotions.

When I talk to you, **Baby**, I always speak the truth. I will never tell you something that is not true.

❦

It is essential to teach children always to speak the truth. Lying causes unclear thinking and can only result in pain and misery. The sure way to teach your child integrity is by always speaking the truth. If you say you will read her a story after her nap, be sure that you do it!

I sleep, but my heart is awake;
It is the voice of my beloved!
Song of Solomon 5:2

I appreciate your crying out to me to let me know when you need me. It is good that you ask me for what you need in your crying voice–the only voice you have. I love your voices, **Baby**.

It may be frustrating for Baby when he wants to express himself, but he has no language with which to speak. Listen to all of the nonverbal signals Baby gives to you, and try to interpret what it is that he wants to say. Simply acknowledging Baby's desire to communicate will help him feel less frustrated.

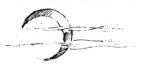

❤ JUNE 26

There is no hurry, **Baby**. Getting big doesn't happen quickly. You cannot eat magic cakes and suddenly be bigger or smaller. I will hold your hand and walk beside you as you grow. You are growing at exactly the right pace.

In the book, <u>Alice In Wonderland</u>, magical things like quickly getting bigger or smaller happen. In real life it takes time to get big, and we can never get small again. Remember, Baby will never ever be exactly as old as she is today. You know your infant as no one else will ever know her. Even Baby will never remember what she was like as a baby. Today, celebrate the awesome privilege of knowing her at this precious moment.

You are beautiful, **Baby**. You are loved. To me, you are the most special little (boy/girl) in the whole world!

<hr>

> *You can give Baby kinesthetic anchors or triggers by saying special words while touching in a specific way. For example: Touch Baby's cheek with a light stroke, smile and tell him he is beautiful and that you love him. This is a neurological imprint. Later when you lightly stroke his cheek, smile at him, and tell him he is beautiful, he may remember the key word "loved" without hearing it.*

Today I am going to sit quietly and let my eyes and smiling face speak to you of my love, **Baby**.

In silence we can experience love. We can demonstrate to Baby that love can be communicated in nonverbal ways.

O that I was where I would be,
Then would I be where I am not.
But where I am I must be,
And where I would be I cannot.

Nursery Rhyme

I love you, **Baby**, even when I cannot be with you.

It is good to tell Baby that some of your time is your own and that you cannot share all of it with her. At the same time, it is important to let Baby know that when you cannot be there, you will make certain that someone else who will provide for her needs will be present. When you are planning to leave Baby with a care-giver, talk about it ahead of time. Name the care-giver, and discuss how that person relates to Baby. Tell Baby something specific you will do together when you get home.

Humpty-Dumpty sat on a wall,
Humpty-Dumpty had a great fall;
All the king's horses, and all the king's men,
Cannot put Humpty-Dumpty together again.

Nursery Rhyme

➤━◆➤━O━◆➤━◄

You are wonderful in all ways. You are smart and beautiful. I love all of you, **Baby**.

Never wound your child with words like "stupid,"
"ugly," "bad," "noisy," etc. Always speak in a kind,
gentle voice, and describe Baby in a positive way.
Tomorrow he will become exactly what you tell him he
is today.

Hot July brings cooling showers,
Apricots and gillyflowers.

Nursery Rhyme

I have faith in you. I have hope for you. My love is dedicated to you, **Baby**. Like July's apricots and gillyflowers, you are God's sweet gift to me and to our family.

I like doing things with you, **Baby**. Each day we have fun together. Each day we bond close together and learn more about each other. I like learning new things about you, **Baby**.

Name the things you and Baby do together in the sequence that you do them. Repeat the order in which daily routines are handled. Try to make the everyday experiences and routines that you and Baby share predictable. When she learns that she can expect certain things, it will give her a sense of security. At the same time, spontaneity once in a while will teach her flexibility.

Count it all joy when you fall into various trials.

James 1:2

I love your voice, **Baby**. What you have to say is important. When I awaken each morning to the sound of your little voice calling me, I am glad to have another day with you. I will always listen to what you want to tell me.

Expect that some days you will feel exhausted from mothering. If at all possible, nap when Baby naps. Take special care of yourself so you can do all that you must do for Baby. Today do something kind and loving for yourself, Mommy.

My country, 'tis of thee,
Sweet land of liberty,
Of thee I sing:
Land where my fathers died,
Land of the pilgrims' pride,
From every mountainside
Let freedom ring.

America

Today we will celebrate, **Baby**. This is the holiday when we celebrate being Americans. We live in a country called America. It is a good place to be born. As you grow, you will learn more about this place where you live called the United States of America.

We live on a beautiful planet called Earth. You are part of the earth, **Baby**. The planet will give you air and water and beauty. It will cradle you always, just as I cradle you while you are a baby.

Earth is full of color. You are the lucky one that will get to show Baby rainbows, roses, green grass and trees, blue skies and seas, pastel pink dawns and red-pepper scarlet sunsets. Your enthusiasm for the beauty of our planet will train him to appreciate it.

Let every man be swift to hear, slow to speak, slow to wrath.

James 1:19

It is good, **Baby**, that you cry to tell me what you need. I understand that you cry because you do not have words to speak that tell me what you want.

Careful listening is a way to honor Baby. You can ease the frustration of her not knowing how to speak by being a patient listener. It may be exasperating for Baby not to be able to communicate her wishes but lots of cuddling can provide the reassurance and nurturing needed for her to feel connected to you. When you listen and respond to Baby, you are validating your love for her.

I love to wrap my arms around you in a big hug. I like it when you hug me back. You can hug me when you need a hug any time you choose. I enjoy hugging you back, **Baby**.

———

You can help Baby acquire basic trust in his own goodness and self-worth by giving him lots and lots of hugs. For babies to be emotionally healthy and happy, they need to be touched and hugged many times each day.

Diddle, diddle, dumpling, my son John,
He went to bed with his stockings on;
One shoe off, one shoe on;
Diddle, diddle, dumpling, my son John.

Nursery Rhyme

You like to look at your feet and hands. They are beautiful, **Baby**. You like to pull (at/off) your socks to see your toes. It is good that you notice these things.

Oh my God, I trust in you....
Psalm 25:2

I trust you, **Baby**. You trust me. God loves us both, you and me. Because God loves us both, we are open to the joys of the universe. There is a lot of love in this world, **Baby**, and I love you.

In order to grow in an emotionally healthy way, babies must feel that they can trust others. The only way babies can learn trust is to experience trustworthy relationships. When you are consistently available to meet Baby's needs, you are teaching her to trust. Holding her in a gentle or loving way will teach her to trust the safety of your arms.

The Queen of Hearts
She made some tarts,
All on a summer's day.

Nursery Rhyme

I will always love you, **Baby**, no matter what season it is or what the weather is like. The season we are having is called summer. The weather in summertime is sunny and hot. Would you like to take a walk and talk about summer?

Early morning or late afternoon walks make summertime a perfect time for exploration. Be cautious when taking Baby out in hot weather. Cover his skin and shield his eyes from direct sunlight.

All of your feelings are okay, **Baby**. I honor all of your feelings, but I do not experience them. Your feelings are yours, they belong to you. My feelings are mine, they belong to me. Even though our feelings are not the same at the same time, we can communicate.

It is good to be connected to Baby, but it is not healthy to be emotionally entangled with her. Just as Baby's sadness does not have to be your sadness, your baby should not have to feel your anger, sorrow, or pain.

Then she made a vow and said,
" O Lord of hosts, if You will indeed....
give your maidservant a male child,
then I will give him to the Lord all the days of his life...."

I Samuel 1:11

You are an answer to my prayers. I love you,
Baby. My life is more complete with you in it.
My world is more whole.

Do you have a fantasy about being "the perfect
mother"? Remember, motherhood will often be a strug-
gle. Accepting that it doesn't have to be what you
dreamed it would be may help you distinguish between
fantasy and realistic expectations. Expecting perfection
will only be setting yourself up for failure. Be proud of
what you are doing and the things you are learning
about being a mother.

I love us both. I will take care of me as well as I take care of you, **Baby**.

Do you think that your own needs are insignificant, Mommy? In the never-ending demands of Baby, do you ignore your own care? If you do, you may become overly exhausted. A tired mother isn't the best mother. To be the very best mom that you can be, take care of your own needs, too. Get a care-giver for Baby today, and spend some quality time doing something you enjoy. You deserve it!

Handy Spandy, Jack a-dandy,
Loves plum-cake and sugar candy;
He bought some at a grocer's shop,
And out he came, hop-hop-hop.

Nursery Rhyme

Baby, you are lovable and deserve to be loved.
Does it feel good when I give you love? You are
learning to give love, too. I will help you learn to
express your love and be affectionate to others. I
love you, **Baby**.

I have spread my dreams under your feet;
Tread softly because you tread on my dreams.

William Butler Yeats

I will help you make some of your dreams come true, **Baby**. I will do whatever I can to help you be the person you want to be. I will give you love and encouragement every day, **Baby**.

What little pictures play in Baby's head when she is dreaming? What things does she wish for while she is awake? Someday she will be able to tell you, and you will be able to help her fulfill her dreams.

Let me dry your tears, **Baby**. Let me end your fears, **Baby**. Baby (girl/boy) I'm here for you because I love you, **Baby**.

Do you sometimes feel sad or blue? Cranky or irritated? Ask yourself, "What would you do for Baby if he felt that way?" The next time you feel depressed, do for yourself what you would do for Baby.

Laugh if you feel like laughing, **Baby**. Cry if you feel like crying. Throw a tantrum if you feel like it. I love you no matter how you feel.

Baby does not know how to release tension in an appropriate way yet. As she gets older, you will show her how to channel negative feelings in acceptable ways. Mommy, how do you handle negative feelings? Here are just a few ways to release tension:

talk to a safe person	*exercise*
drink herb tea	*play soft music*
take a walk or run	*dance or sing*
look at photographs	*read a good book*
hit a pillow with your fist	*have a good cry*
take a candlelight bath	*join a group*
watch an old movie	*read poetry*

Welcome to today! I am here to make things the best for you that I possibly can. I care about your happiness, **Baby**. You are lovable and deserve to be happy.

Do you feel trapped by the past? Are you afraid that you will make the same parenting mistakes that your parents made with you? If your childhood was negative, you can learn from yesterday. Forgive the past, and change the present by practicing positive parenting.

❤ July 19

You mean so much to me, **Baby**. You make my life better and brighter. I love you. I can't imagine what life was like before you came, **Baby**. You have enriched my life with your presence.

Do you ever think your words to Baby are "much ado about nothing"? Although Baby will not remember each of your words, he will never forget the feeling of love he experiences when you speak to him in gentle, loving ways.

Heigh, diddle, diddle,
The cat and the fiddle,
The cow jumped over the moon;
The little dog laughed
To see such sport,
And the dish ran away with the spoon.

Nursery Rhyme

Someday when you are bigger, **Baby**, and can better understand, I'll tell you about things much bigger than you and I. I'll tell you stories about the beautiful lights in the night sky, the great moon, and arches of colors above called rainbows. Ask me when you are curious, and I will answer.

I like your little drools, **Baby**. You cannot
control your swallows perfectly yet, so you
dribble little bits of wetness. I think it is sweet
that your tiny chin is wet sometimes. Someday
you will not drool, and I will miss these days.

*Appreciate every single thing about Baby. Talk about all
of her body functions (burping, spitting up, etc.). Let
her know that they are all okay. Love Baby for all of the
things she is and for all of the things she is not.*

Be patient....
James 5:7

I love all of the moments we spend together, **Baby**. I enjoy getting to know you and watching you grow. The times I spend with you are the most special moments of my life. I will be especially patient with you today and always. My love for you will never end.

Time is the true test of love. Be patient. As the years go by and your love for Baby grows and grows, he will learn to trust love, and trust you, and trust himself. He will gain the courage needed to claim what he loves.

Birds of a feather flock together,
And so will pigs and swine;
Rats and mice will have their choice,
And so will I have mine.

Nursery Rhyme

The world is a good place. There is so much to look forward to, **Baby**. Someday I'll show you the creatures of the earth who share our planet. There are beautiful birds that soar through the sky, squirrels that live in trees, bears that sleep in caves, zebras that graze in meadows, monkeys that swing from trees, rabbits that scurry underground. Someday you may have your own pet.

Does your family have a pet? Talk to Baby about your family animal. Explain that all baby animals have a mother. Tell Baby how some animals give their babies milk. Talk about how all baby animals start out being very small and grow bigger.

"Come, let's to bed,"
Says Sleepy-head;
"Tarry a while," says Slow.
"Put on the pot,"
Says the Greedy one,
"Let's sup before we go."
Nursery Rhyme

I am glad that you are here. I love you, **Baby**.
Let's spend a quiet moment together before you
go to sleep. I am glad that tomorrow is another
day that we will share.

Today we fill our lives with memories of each other. I love who you are today, **Baby**. I love who you are going to grow up to be. Someday we will look back upon today and the happiness we shared together.

If you have photographs of Baby, show them to him. Show him photographs of familiar people and the family pet(s). Show him photographs of you when you were a baby.

A swarm of bees in May
Is worth a load of hay;
A swarm of bees in June
Is worth a silver spoon;
A swarm of bees in July
Is not worth a fly.

Nursery Rhyme

You do not have to fit into my schedule right now, **Baby**. You have your own schedule. I will honor it. You are growing at exactly the right pace. I am willing to slow down and go at baby-step pace so I can go along with you. I love you, **Baby**.

I love to watch you play, **Baby**. Do you like to watch me? I do many tasks each day, and other people have tasks, too. There are many things that need to be done to meet each family member's needs. Families work together to help each other.

Name your daily tasks. Name family members, and describe how each contributes to the family. Your attitude toward daily tasks will send a clear message to Baby. If you sing or smile and appear happy while you work, Baby will learn that even routine tasks can be performed with joy.

See, see. What shall I see?
A horse's head where his tail should be.

Nursery Rhyme

✻

You have beautiful eyes and beautiful ears, **Baby**.
You can see and you can hear.

You can enhance Baby's visual and auditory perceptions
by playing looking and listening games. Describe the
color, size, and shape of a few objects in the room and
the sounds made by others. It doesn't matter whether
she can understand your words or not. When you
present words with objects she can see or sounds she
can hear, it is easier for her to make the connection
between the word and the object.

My heart is steadfast....
I will sing....I will awaken the dawn.
Psalm 57:7,8

Would you like to hear a song? Would you like to hear a story? I want to entertain you today. We can have some fun singing and reading. I love our time together, **Baby**.

Acknowledge the sounds Baby makes as songs and stories. He is talking to you in a very special language of love. The more you listen, the more he will express himself.

I promise to be there always to comfort you, **Baby.** You won't always like every single thing that happens, but you can trust that I will be there to help you through difficult times.

Are you keeping up with Baby's immunizations? Check Baby's Personal Immunization Chart in the back of this book. If Baby needs an immunization, don't delay. Make the necessary appointment today.

Little Tommy Grace
Had a pain in his face,
So bad he could not learn a letter;
When in came Dicky Long,
Singing such a funny song,
That Tommy laughed,
And found his face much better.

Nursery Rhyme

Growing is fun, **Baby**. As you grow, you will have more and more freedom to play at things you choose. Playing is good and fun. Someday you will have many toys, and you will know how to run and choose what you want to do next.

Make sure Baby has his own appropriate toys: books with board, cloth, or vinyl pages; unbreakable mirrors; colorful mobiles; rattles, music boxes, and other toys that make noises; small stuffed animals, pliable balls, and soft pillows.

214

You are unique and special, **Baby**. Watching you, I sometimes see hints of me in your face. Your features reflect many members of our family. You are part of a big family and long history of ancestors. But at the same time, **Baby**, you are unlike anyone else who has ever been born. I love your uniqueness.

Tell Baby about certain physical features that she shares with family members. Name the feature and tell her whom it resembles. This process will build strong family connections.

One, two, buckle my shoe;
Three, four, shut the door;
Five, six, pick up sticks;
Seven, eight, lay them straight;
Nine, ten, a good fat hen.

Nursery Rhyme

＊═◉═＊

You are smart, **Baby**. You are learning new
words every day. Do you want to play a game?
We can count. We can play a touching game. I
love to play with you.

Play a touching game with Baby. Say: "See your shoe?
Touch your shoe. See the door? Let's touch the door."
Name things in the room, and carry Baby over and let
Baby feel each one. You can guide his hand, or you can
touch it as you say it.

Twinkle, twinkle, little star,
How I wonder what you are!
Up above the world so high,
Like a diamond in the sky.

Nursery Rhyme

Go to sleep, my baby. Happy dreams! I love you as many ways as there are stars in the sky. I will love you for as long as the sky has stars and a moon and whirling planets. I will love you forever, **Baby**.

August brings the sheaves of corn,
Then the harvest home is borne.

Nursery Rhyme

You are getting bigger every day, **Baby**. I like to watch you grow. You are exactly the right size.

It doesn't matter if Baby is either larger or smaller than other babies his age. The important thing is to watch his rate of growth. You may want to keep track of his weight and length on the growth charts at the back of this book.

Onery, ooery ickery Ann
Fillacy, follacy Nicholas John,
Quivy, Quavy English navy,
Striggleum, Straggleum, buck!
Nursery Rhyme

Baby, **Baby**, I hope you like your name. Your name was chosen just for you. I like the sound of your name. Your name belongs to you. Your name will always be special to me because it is your name.

Tell Baby who chose her name, and describe the circumstances. If she was named after someone, show her photographs of that person. Tell her all about her namesake.

True life is lived when tiny changes occur.

Tolstoy

You are becoming the person you are meant to be, **Baby**. Each "step" that you take in your growing will empower you. Growing is a gradual process. There is no hurry for you to learn to walk or talk or take care of yourself. I welcome doing these things for you. As you learn to do each one, I will celebrate with you.

A glass of milk and a slice of bread,
And then good-night, we must go to bed.

Nursery Rhyme

I promise to provide you with food for your body and love to nourish your spirit. I promise to provide a safe place for you to learn and create your future. I promise to love you always, **Baby**.

"Mother, may I go out to swim?"
"Yes, my darling daughter:
Hang your clothes on a hickory limb
And don't go near the water."

Nursery Rhyme

If I seem to hold you too close and too tight, it is because I love you so. I am learning to be a mother as you are learning to be a child. We are sharing a unique learning experience. I love you, **Baby**.

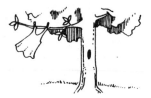

A student is not above his teacher,
but everyone who is fully trained
will be like his teacher.
Luke 6:40

>‹

I am honored to be your first teacher, **Baby**.
You will have many more teachers during your
lifetime. In fact, most persons that you meet may
have something to teach you. I will help you
learn how to be open to learning and how to recognize a good teacher.

Nose, nose, jolly red nose;
And what gave you that jolly red nose?
Nutmegs and cinnamon, spices and clovers,
And they gave me this jolly red nose.

Nursery Rhyme

There are many wonderful things for you to discover! I have noticed that you seem to enjoy certain aromas, **Baby**. Soon you will discover numerous and delicious scents. You will smell flowers, chocolates, warm ginger cookies, and rain on the grass. Everything has a scent, and soon you will discover them all!

Does Baby's little nose curl up and sniff when he smells milk? Often infants can recognize the scent of their own mother's breast milk. You can teach Baby to appreciate the wonderful aromatic world by pointing out to him how things smell and letting him know that you value your sense of smell. If it isn't too hot today, take Baby for a walk so he can enjoy the smells of the outdoors.

For God is not the author of confusion, but of peace.

I Corinthians 14:33

Everything is okay, **Baby**. I will try to provide a harmonious place for you to grow. I will try to provide serene circumstances and peaceful times for you to enrich your spirit. We will have many quiet times together.

> *Do not abuse Baby by requiring her to exist in chaos. Provide a calm, serene place for her to grow. If there are a lot of people in your family and your home is small, find quiet retreats where you and Baby can get away. Turn off the television and radios and make feeding times as quiet as possible.*

Let's have fun, **Baby**, and do something unexpected today. Let's do something we have never
done before. Let's explore the possibilities of the
day.

———

*Think about something new and exciting that you can
do with Baby. Tell him about your plans, and go do
them. An unexpected excursion is great for breaking the
routine. Spontaneity will make mothering more enjoyable for you, and it will help Baby learn to adapt to the
many changes he will face in the future.*

If I had a donkey that wouldn't go,
Would I wallop him? Oh, no, no!

Nursery Rhyme

You are learning to be gentle and kind, **Baby**. You and I are part of an intricate chain of family relationships that has a long history and will go on for generations and generations.

Remember that Baby will someday treat others the way you are treating her today. The patterns you set now will live on long after you are no longer on earth. The gentle, kind ways you teach Baby will be taught to her babies and their babies and their babies.

You are learning to think! Once you only let me know when you were comfortable and uncomfortable, but now you are learning ways to communicate all kinds of messages. Your smile tells me that you are happy. I love you, **Baby**.

When Baby shakes a rattle and it makes a certain sound, she will learn from that. Baby will learn that other objects make different and interesting sounds, too. Soon she will begin banging things on the floor or dropping them over the edge of her bed or high chair to hear the sound they make when they crash on the floor. Provide unbreakable toys so she can experiment and learn from her play.

How many days has my baby to play?
Saturday, Sunday, Monday,
Tuesday, Wednesday, Thursday, Friday,
Saturday, Sunday, Monday.

Nursery Rhyme

You are eager to reach out and touch and explore the world around you. I love to watch you smile, laugh, babble, and play. You are having fun every day. You are growing, **Baby**.

Play is every child's work. Help Baby learn to play. Humans who do not learn how to play when they are children have difficulty playing or enjoying themselves as adults.

Where have you been all the day,
My boy, Willy?
Where have you been all the day,
My boy Willy?

Nursery Rhyme

I love to play with you, **Baby**. Let's play a looking game. Let's look at your toys. Let's play peekaboo.

Infants believe that things disappear when they cannot see them. If you hide a toy behind your back, Baby may think that it has vanished forever. When you play games like peekaboo, Baby will learn that objects have permanence. Play games to teach Baby about permanency. Say: "See your toy?" (Hide it behind your back.) "Now do you see it? Where did it go? Here it is!" (Show him the toy.) "Let's play this game some more. Do you see your toy?" (Repeat.)

You are becoming who you are meant to be, **Baby**. You are developing your own personality as more and more of your basic nature emerges. I accept all of your characteristics. I will not try to change you or mold you into what I think you should be. I will encourage you to be who you are. I love you exactly as you are, **Baby**.

As you watch Baby's personality developing, it may surprise or even shock you. He may be rambunctious or easygoing, cranky or joy-filled, strong-willed or compliant. Temperaments are believed to be inborn character traits. Although you may not find each of his characteristics pleasing to you, it is best to adapt to them and not try to change his basic nature. Unconditional love will give him permission to become exactly who he is meant to be.

Where should a baby rest?
Where but on its mother's arm--
Where can a baby lie
Half so safe from every harm?
Nursery Rhyme

———•———

Go to sleep my beautiful baby, **Baby**. I know that sometimes it is hard for you to go to sleep. I will be patient and help you relax so you can sleep.

If Baby is especially alert and active during the day, unwinding at night may sometimes be difficult. Have you tried giving her a warm bath, rocking her and singing a lullaby, massaging her back, or playing soft music for her? If over a period of time you repeat the same method to help her relax, eventually she will associate that activity with going to sleep.

Sing a song of sixpence,
A pocket full of rye,
Four and twenty blackbirds
Baked in a pie;
When the pie was opened,
The birds began to sing;
Wasn't that a dainty dish
To set before a king?

Nursery Rhyme

Looking at birds is fun. You know how to look and see new things. You are smart, **Baby**. Each day will bring new challenges and triumphs for you, **Baby**. You will see wonderful new birds each season of the year.

Go outside on an adventure to find a bird. Say: "Birds are all sizes and all colors. They can fly and walk on the ground. Do you think we can see a big bird? Can we see a black bird? Let's go look for birds!"

You have a wonderful smile, **Baby**. See my teeth? Let's look at your pretty mouth. Your smile is nice. All the parts of your face are beautiful.

If Baby has teeth, use a hand mirror to show him his teeth. Teething usually begins between four and eight months. Teething can cause a low-grade temperature, excessive drooling, irritability, and crying spells. You can help ease Baby's discomfort by gently massaging his gums with one of your fingers or letting him chew on a cold (not frozen) teething ring.

You are a good baby, **Baby**. Sometimes you may want to do things that would cause you pain or be dangerous, and I will have to stop you. I am here to teach you and keep you safe. Trust that when I say, "No," it is for your own good. I will try to say, "Yes," most of the time.

The best way to deal with Baby's trying to do something she shouldn't do is to distract her. Redirect her attention to another activity. Never spank or punish Baby. Babies cannot make the connection between misbehavior and punishment. The only thing a baby can learn from being punished is that the world is not always a safe place and that sometimes you bring her pain.

So the child grew and was weaned.
And Abraham made a great feast
on the same day that Isaac was weaned.

Genesis 21:8

I celebrate you today, **Baby**. Someday we will have parties, and we will invite your friends to come and celebrate your special days. We will blow up balloons and wear hats and sing songs. There will be bright colored packages with bows and cards. We will celebrate all of your growing with friends and feasts.

Enjoy Baby today. Spend time laughing and singing and kissing and hugging. Cuddling Baby is like milk for his spirit. It will nourish him and help him grow strong emotionally. And it will be healthy for you too, Mommy.

Rejoice, O young man, in your youth,
And let your heart cheer you in the days of your youth.

Ecclesiastes 11:9

➤─◆─○─◆─◄

I like to watch you, **Baby**. Sometimes I will allow you to struggle so that you can discover for yourself, and other times I will come to your rescue. Whatever I do, **Baby**, I love you.

Mommy, sometimes it will be hard to distinguish the difference between the things that challenge Baby and the things that frustrate him. He won't learn if you jump in to assist too soon, and he won't explore if learning is a painful experience. You will soon become the best judge of what is a challenge and what is impossible for Baby.

You are learning to do many new things all by yourself. You can (name the things Baby can do). You are smart, **Baby**. I am proud of you!

Can Baby crawl yet? Becoming mobile will make an enormous difference in her safety. Moving about will empower her and give her new freedom, but be cautious because she can quickly get into dangerous situations. Take time out to double-check and make sure that your house is baby-proof.

For you meet him with the blessings of goodness;
You set a crown of pure gold upon his head.

Psalm 21:3

I love you, **Baby**. Today I will trust in my own goodness as your mother. My gift to you is my sincere efforts to be present and open to you.

Cling to what is good.

Romans 12:9

I am here for you, **Baby**. I will keep you safe. Sometimes you may feel shy around strangers. It is okay that you want to cling to me when you feel frightened of unfamiliar people or objects.

> *Don't concern yourself if Baby is shy around strangers. It is good that he can tell the difference between familiar and unfamiliar people. His shyness is evidence of his healthy relationship with you and other familiar people.*

I like to be with you, **Baby**. I know that you like to be with me. You sometimes feel sad when we are separated. I must leave you sometimes, but I will always come back to you.

⚜

At eight to eighteen months, many babies experience separation anxiety. Baby's attachment to you may cause her to cry when you leave her. Keep in mind that she thinks you are the most wonderful, beautiful, extraordinary person in the whole world. Not having you near can be painful for her. Reassure her each time you leave, that you will return soon. For most babies, the fear of separation usually disappears before the age of three.

Swan swam over the sea;
Swim, swan, swim.
Swan swam back again;
Well swum, swan.

Nursery Rhyme

Do you like your bath, **Baby**? You like to play in the warm, wet, play place. Here are some toys, and you can play in the bath while I support you and help you get clean. Someday you will learn to swim and dive and play in the (sea/lake/pool).

Open your hearts to us.
II Corinthians 7:2

I will never abandon you, **Baby**. I will always be here for you. No matter how old you are, you will always be welcome in my house. There will always be a safe place for you in my heart.

Did you know that fear of being abandoned begins in the first seconds of life? Baby doesn't know when you leave if she will ever see you again. Only in the coming and going, coming and going, can she learn to trust that you will always return.

You have many needs, **Baby**. Today I will meet all of your needs for you. That is my job. I am your parent. Someday you will be big and capable of meeting all of your own needs.

Teach Baby that eventually he will become responsible for meeting his own needs. As he grows and you help identify his needs and meet each one, you are sending him a clear message that you love him while demonstrating how needs are met.

Play, play every day,
Harry throws his time away.
He must work and he must read,
And then he'll be a man indeed.

Nursery Rhyme

Playing is good. You have a special toy. I think it is your favorite. Let's play with your special toy together. I like to be with you, **Baby**.

Get the toy that you think is Baby's favorite and embrace it in an accepting way. If you cherish her favorite toy, it will make it even more special to her.

A wife of noble character who can find?
She is worth far more than rubies...
Her children arise and call her blessed;
Her husband also, and he praises her.

Proverbs 31:10,28

You teach me many things, **Baby**. You have taught me to love myself for I sometimes see myself reflected in your gaze. Today I will try to view myself through your eyes. I will give myself the unconditional love that you generously give to me.

You have many responsibilities as a mother. In order to meet all of Baby's needs, you will need to stay healthy and happy. Be especially kind to yourself today. See yourself as the extraordinary human being that Baby sees when he lovingly gazes at you.

To market, to market, to buy a plum cake,
Home again, home again, market is late.
To market, to market, to buy a plum bun,
Home again, home again, market is done.

Nursery Rhyme

Today is a new day full of opportunities for closeness. I will be gentle with you and gentle with
myself, too. I love you, **Baby**.

I will lead on slowly at a pace....
the children, are able to endure....

Genesis 33:14

You can trust in me, **Baby**. I am your teacher and friend. It feels good to know that I am capable of being your guide. You can put your hand in mine, and trust me to safely lead you along your journey to adulthood.

It will give Baby a secure feeling to know that you are there and will guide her. Invite her often to hold your hand. Touching Baby provides her with the physical connection that she needs to grow emotionally healthy.

Warm September brings the fruit,
Nursery Rhyme

You have all the time in the world to do your growing. You can trust that I am watching over you, **Baby**. With each passing day you are growing at exactly the right speed.

As seasons change, so does Baby. Everyday you will see Baby doing different and new things. Talk to her about all of the ways she is changing. Praise her as she reaches each milestone.

❤ SEPTEMBER 5

You are beautiful, healthy, happy, and strong, **Baby**. I am always near to hear your sobs and dry your tears. Like a friendly sparrow, when need be, I will cheer you on and tell you to exert yourself.

In Beatrix Potter's book, Peter Rabbit, when Peter gave himself up for lost, he shed big tears. When some friendly sparrows heard his sobs, they told him to "exert" himself. Sometimes when mothering seems overwhelming, remember the sparrows' advice, and exert yourself!

I value you, **Baby**. I value everything about you.
With my gentle touches, I honor you with love
and respect.

---

*Baby will learn to value others by being valued. He will
learn to be gentle by being handled in gentle ways. He
will learn to love and respect others because he is loved
and respected.*

When Jesus saw their faith, he said...
"Son, be of good cheer."
Matthew 9:2

You are unique and unlimited. You are alive with love and joy. You are free to be all that you can be. I love you, **Baby**.

> *Be Baby's cheerleader and encourage her in all of her development. Applaud every new thing that she learns to do. Chant your praises when she expresses joy.*

I am glad that I am your mother. You are a very special baby, **Baby**. For now, being your mother is my most important work.

⊶⇒○⇐⊷

Some days it may seem that your parenting path is narrow, dark, and fraught with stumbling blocks. Mothering isn't easy. It may shed some light on your path to meditate on the joy Baby brings to you.

One misty, moisty morning,
When cloudy was the weather,
I chanced to meet an old man clothed all in leather.
He began to compliment, and I began to grin,
How do you do, and how do you do?
And how do you do again?

Nursery Rhyme

You are terrific, **Baby**. Rest assured in my care. I will keep you wrapped safely in my arms of love. I will give you the warmth of my smile.

A compliment can brighten even a misty, moisty, cloudy morning. A smile can change the weather from gloomy gray to bright, sunny blue.

When the morning stars sang together,
And all the sons of God shouted for joy
Psalm 38:7

I am pleased with all of your growth. It is good that you are learning to feel wonderful about yourself, **Baby**. You make me so happy that I often feel like singing!

It is essential for Baby to learn to love himself. The way you treat him will teach him whether or not he is lovable. Always keep in mind that the way you treat him today may be the way he will treat himself for his entire lifetime.

Love your own, kiss your own,
Love your own mother....
Nursery Rhyme

I love to hug you, **Baby**. Touching you and loving you makes me very happy, too.

Touch Baby many times each day in an affirming way. You might use a hug, a gentle touch, or a back rub. Being touched will help Baby develop a positive self-image while teaching her how to nurture others.

Cry, baby, cry,
Put your finger in your eye,
And tell your mother it wasn't I.
Nursery Rhyme

❧

I'll dry your tears. I'll calm your fears, **Baby**.
Mother is near. Mother will hold you and
cuddle you and make you feel safe.

Do you suffer guilt and avoid outings because Baby cries
when you go? Mommy, the tears will stop as soon as
you leave. Baby is crying to persuade you to stay with
him. When you are out of sight, he will see that the
tears didn't work, and he will soon stop crying. Get out
without Baby today.

Butterfly, butterfly, from where do you come?
I know not, I ask not, I never had a home.
Butterfly, butterfly, where do you go?
Where the sun shines, and where the buds grow.

Nursery Rhyme

▶━◀▸━O━◂▸━◀

You are safe, **Baby**. I know that new faces sometimes frighten you. I will let you know who is safe. I won't allow strangers to frighten you. I will help you make new friends.

You can ease some of Baby's fear of new faces by insisting that people spend time warming up to her. Don't let strangers scoop up Baby or come close too quickly. Slow and gentle introductions will help her feel more secure with unfamiliar faces.

You enjoy food, **Baby**. The world is full of good things to eat. Soon you will enjoy many new delicious flavors: crunchy red apples, squishy green peas, soft orange yams, and sweet brown chocolates, jam sandwiches, warm apple pie, tangy pasta, and orange juice. Food is great fun.

❧

Early stages of self-feeding are often exciting for baby but frustrating for Mommy. Try feeding Baby most of his food, and then let him finish the meal with finger foods: crunchy toast, scrambled eggs, avocado bits, or tiny chunks of ripe banana. Later you can introduce foods that Baby can eat with a spoon: oatmeal, cooked strained fruits, mashed egg yolk, cottage cheese, yogurt, tofu, rice, mashed potato, pudding, baby food. Avoid foods that can cause choking: popcorn, peanuts, hot dogs, hard candies, dry cereals, and peanut butter.

Sing, sing! What shall I sing?
The cat's run away with the pudding-bag string!
Nursery Rhyme

Learning to play is fun, **Baby**. I will teach you
how I play. Later you will have your own special
ways to play.

When Baby can sit up on her own, provide appropriate
toys: stacking toys like blocks, cups, and unbreakable
containers; toys with moving parts like busy boxes,
squeeze toys, vehicle toys of flexible plastic, and a toy
telephone; and books with plastic or vinyl pages. You
can show Baby how to play with toys. Say: "Watch me
stack these blocks. Now I am going to knock them
down. I will stack them again. Do you want to knock
them down this time?"

You can trust me to take good care of you, **Baby**.
Caring for you is something I take seriously. I
know that all of your needs are significant.

> *When infants receive trustworthy handling, they*
> *develop a strong sense of trust. If care-giving is chaotic*
> *or inconsistent, babies may develop a deep sense of dis-*
> *trust, insecurity, and low self-esteem.*

We can take turns singing cooing songs whenever you choose. I will sing soft lullabies for you. I will give you a turn to sing softly back to me. I love you, **Baby**.

Play singing or interaction games such as peekaboo or pat-a-cake with Baby. When talking softly to Baby, give him a turn to respond in his cooing voice. When he does, reinforce it with more cooing songs. Listen again. Soon you will be having a "conversation."

Mary, Mary, quite contrary,
How does your garden grow?
Silver bells and cockle shells,
And pretty maids all in a row.

Nursery Rhyme

I love you, **Baby**. I respect you, **Baby**. I admire you, **Baby**. Every part of you is lovable. I accept all of you.

When Baby is admired and loved unconditionally, she will grow to be an adult with a deep holistic feeling of self-worth. Every word you speak to Baby is like watering a plant. She is thirsty for your attention; she is hungry for your love. Attention and love nourish her spirit and will make her bloom.

Peace be multiplied to you...
and steadfast forever...
He delivers and rescues.

Daniel 6:2-27

You are safe, **Baby**. I'll be there for you when darkness falls. I'll chase away your nightmares and hold you until you are no longer afraid. I will be your light in the darkness of night and rescue you when you need me.

What are little girls made of?
Sugar and spice, and everything nice;
That's what little girls are made of.

Nursery Rhyme

I am glad you are a (boy/girl). You are sweet and everything about you is nice. I wouldn't change anything about you. You are exactly, perfectly you. I love you, **Baby**.

I thank my God upon every remembrance of you.
Philippians 1:3

I am so grateful that you are in my life. I thank God for you every day. You are a wonderful blessing. When we are not together, my thoughts of you bring me happiness, **Baby**.

Many of my waking hours are spent with you.
My life has changed since you were born. I like
the changes. I like being with you, **Baby**!

Even though you enjoy spending time and energy caring
for Baby, don't neglect your own needs. Don't abandon
old friends or hobbies. Balance your life by including
some of the things that brought you pleasure before
Baby arrived.

And Jesus....took a little child and set him by Him,
and said to them,
"Whoever receives this little child in my name receives me;
and whoever receives me receives Him who sent me.
For he who is least among you all will be great."

Luke 9:48

I will care for you, **Baby**. Trust that the earth is a safe place for you to grow and learn. God will hold you safely in His love, while I cradle you in my arms.

Baby will learn trust when it is something he can feel, like being cuddled in your secure arms. Your touches will send a strong message to him about trust, safety, and love.

The bunnies all sleep soundly,
Beneath the moon's bright ray;
They nod their heads together,
And dream the night away.

Nursery rhyme

It is sweet to see you sleeping, **Baby**. I like to listen to your soft breath and see your tiny body moving as you inhale and exhale. Even as you sleep, you bring joy to others.

Today I will give you all that I can give, **Baby**. I will be open to the joy you bring to me. I will be still and listen to your sweet cooing songs and gurgles.

Just let go of any of your own troubles or self-pity you have today, and be open to the joy you share with Baby.

I am thankful for you, **Baby**. There is much to be grateful for today. The life we share is full of good things.

Name some good things that you and Baby share. In her beginning, Baby only sees the world through your eyes. Your attitude will set the examples for how Baby sees the world for the rest of her life. If you are never happy or grateful, she won't learn how to be grateful either. But if you are positive and see life as good, she will grow feeling positive about her world.

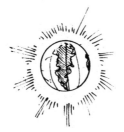

You are here with me, and I am here with you. I will not think about anything right now except experiencing this precious moment with you. I love you, **Baby**.

> *If you live only in the future, anxiously planning and dreaming , or waste time worrying about or missing the past, you will miss the joy of today. Let today be a here-and-now day with Baby.*

....A good tree does not bear bad fruit,
nor does a bad tree bear good fruit.

Luke 6:43

I love you, **Baby**. I have always loved you. I loved you at your conception. I loved you as I carried you within me before you had understanding or knowing. I loved you as you were being born. I love you every day as you are growing. I love you today, and I will love you forever.

Your face is full of joy. Your whole body is full of love. I like to watch you play. I like to play with you, **Baby**.

⇥+⇤

As Baby gets older, he will become more alert and mobile. Create some games that will encourage his self-expression. Try covering him with a light, see-through scarf and ask, "Where is Baby?" Then slowly pull off the scarf and act surprised to see him. Repeat. Soon Baby will learn how to play by pulling off the scarf to reveal himself.

....Peace be to you,
peace to your house,
and peace to all that you have!

I Samuel 25:6

I will never leave you for very long, **Baby**. I know that sometimes you do not like it when I must leave you. I know that it makes you sad. Sometimes it makes me sad, too. But when I go, I will always come back.

Does Baby act shy or anxious around strangers? Does she cry when you leave the room? Does her fearfulness in some situations worry you? Try to keep in mind that separation anxieties are normal feelings.

Go to bed Tom, go to bed Tom,
Merry or sober, go to bed Tom.

Nursery Rhyme

I respect your right to have a favorite (toy/blanket). I know that cuddling this (toy/blanket) brings you security. I am glad that you can comfort yourself when I cannot be there for you. You are already learning how to meet your own needs. I am proud of you, **Baby**.

> *If Baby doesn't already have a favorite security object to use for coping with stress, encourage him to choose one by placing a small, soft blanket or toy in his crib. Don't worry if at first he ignores it. Eventually he will use the toy that you have placed in his crib, or choose his own object that he likes to sleep with.*

You are curious. That is good, **Baby**. You like to play with everything that you can reach. I cannot always allow you to touch everything that you want to touch. Some things are dangerous and may hurt you. Some things break and they are not yours to break. Sometimes I will say, "No."

※

Telling Baby, "No," and denying her something she wants may be difficult for both of you. But she cannot jeopardize her safety or damage valuable property just because she wants to. When you teach her that sometimes she will not get to do something that she wants very badly to do, that is the first step in her learning self-control.

I will listen for the hidden messages in your cries, **Baby.** I know that your need for attention and validation is as great as your need for food and water.

If you hear a cry that you don't understand or have never heard before, and you don't know what Baby wants, don't be alarmed. He may not even know what he wants. Cuddling him might make both of you feel better. Sometimes he will cry and there is nothing you can give him or do for him that will make him stop. Simply hold him and allow him to have a good cry.

You are smart, **Baby**. You like to explore. I know that you like to put everything into your mouth. That is how you test things to see what they are. I will give you delicious foods to sample.

Give Baby interesting things to taste and keep unsafe things out of her reach. Watch to make sure that she puts only clean and safe things up to her mouth. Don't give her hard pieces of food. Don't leave small objects in her crawling area. Never store medicines or household cleaning products in low places. Put safety latches on drawers and cupboards that contain dangerous or poisonous objects. Place plastic plugs in electrical outlets.

There was an old woman who lived in a shoe,
She had so many children, she didn't know what to do.
She gave them some broth, without any bread,
She whipped them all round, and sent them to bed.

Nursery Rhyme

You are loved, sweet **Baby**. My smile will tell you a hundred times a day that I love you! No matter how busy I may be, my love for you will never change.

Beloved, now we are children of God....
I John 3:2

Baby, you can be who you are. I will always support you. It is okay to learn to do things in your own way and in your own time. I am willing to be with you no matter what. I love you, **Baby**.

You are teaching Baby about who she is. You are helping her discover her identity. It is empowering to have an identity. You are giving her the gift to live a courageous life and to know who she is.

He who tiptoes cannot stand,
He who strides cannot walk.

Chinese Proverb

❖❖❖

You are courageous, **Baby**. I will stay close to you when you begin to test your boundaries and discover your limits. It is good that you are learning to think for yourself. I love watching you grow.

I have shown you in every way,
by laboring like this,
that you must support the weak.

Acts 20:35

I love your life energy, **Baby**. It is okay to feel all of your feelings. It is okay to laugh and to cry. It is okay to express your anger and your misery and your fear. It is okay to explore. I support all of you and every feeling that you are having!

Support all of Baby--even his sad feelings. Verbally val-
idate all that he is and all that he is feeling. The words
you speak are his reality. You literally create his emo-
tional environment.

You are uneasy;
you never sailed with me before, I see.
Andrew Jackson

I will keep you safe and guide you, **Baby**. I am calm; I am steady. I will give you balance. Have no fear; don't be uneasy. I will watch over you and look out for you, and teach you to care for yourself.

Fresh October brings the pheasant.
Then to gather nuts is pleasant.

Nursery Rhyme

>‹

I love to play games with you, **Baby**. Playing is how we learn. Do you want to play a shaking hands game?

Play this game with Baby:
Hello! Shaking hands is getting to know you better.
Shaking hands is a greeting of love.
(Shake hands with Baby.)
Hello! Kissing is a nice joining together.
I kiss you, and you kiss me.
(Kiss Baby.)
Good bye. I wave to you, and you wave back.
Waving is sweet parting.
(Wave to Baby.)
Shake hands. Kiss. Wave good-bye.
(Do all three quickly over and over.)

He who is slow to wrath has great understanding,
But he who is impulsive exalts folly.

Proverbs 14:29

❄

Baby, you know what you want. That is good.
It is okay to want things. I will make sure that
you will get what you need, but you won't always
get what you want. But it is okay to want things
you cannot have anyway.

As Baby gets older, he will learn how to let you know
what he wants by gesturing. He may point his little
finger or look at the object he wants. After he lets you
know what he wants, if you don't give it to him, don't
be surprised if he throws a tantrum. Actually this is an
appropriate reaction for an infant. Don't punish him or
scold him. Calm Baby with your soothing words, but
don't give in and give him what he threw a tantrum to
get. If he learns that tantrums work, he will continue
this obnoxious behavior through childhood and into
adulthood. If, instead, he learns that tantrums never
work, he will soon abandon the tactic.

Everything is okay, **Baby**. Don't be afraid if you see that I am sad or angry. I can have feelings that are mine. I can be sad, and it doesn't mean that I am sad because of something you have done. My feelings are separate from you. I always love you, **Baby**, even when I am sad or angry or sick or tired.

Baby cannot comprehend the concept of being separate from you and your feelings, but it is okay to tell her this anyway. If you say it often enough--and mean it--she will be able to grow knowing that she isn't responsible for your feelings. Later she will grow to understand that she isn't responsible for anyone else's feelings either. That will give her the freedom to have functional relationships with others.

Up street, and down street,
Each window's made of glass;
If you go to Tommy Tickler's house,
You'll find a pretty lass.

Nursery Rhyme

———◆———

I am glad that we can be together today. Let's do something new, **Baby**. Let's think of something we have never done before. Let's go up the street and down the street to some place we have never been before.

Tell Baby your idea and go do it. For some adults, being spontaneous is difficult. Is it difficult for you? The only way Baby can learn the joy of spontaneity is to experience it with you. Balance your routines with occasional spontaneity. Routines will teach him security, while spontaneity will teach him to be open and creative and to experience life in a fun-filled way.

I love you in the autumn, **Baby**. In the autumn
the leaves turn colors and fall from the trees.
Let's take a walk and talk about the changes that
we see.

*Point out the seasonal sights to Baby. Your excitement
about life and the changes in the season will be conta-
gious. If you celebrate changes in the weather, she will
learn that change is part of life and not threatening. She
will grow courageously and meet the challenge of
change as a glorious part of being alive.*

Yaup, yaup, yaup!
Said the Frog, as it hopped away;
"The insects feed
On the floating weed,
And I'm hungry for dinner today."
Nursery Rhyme

Baby, I like to feed you. I enjoy bathing you and changing you and keeping you nice and clean. I cherish the time we spend together. You are important. I love you, **Baby**.

> *But when you do good and suffer,*
> *if you take it patiently,*
> *this is commendable....*
>
> I Peter 2:20

I like being your mother. Being your mother is the most important job that I have. It is hard work sometimes, but it is one of the most enjoyable and challenging things that I have ever done. I like you, **Baby**.

Patience is a difficult lesson to learn. If in the past you have lived at an accelerated pace, and now suddenly you have to go at baby-speed, you may find it frustrating. It is okay to feel anxious sometimes. Today be patient with yourself as you learn patience with Baby.

I love you, **Baby**. You matter. I am thankful for
the opportunity to show you how much you
mean to me. I am grateful that I get to share
your growing season.

Baby thirsts and craves to be loved. He needs to feel
connected to someone and know that he is important.
The way you can demonstrate that he is important is to
treat him with love and gentleness. If you are always
there to meet his needs, he knows that he matters to
you. If you tell him that you love him, it reinforces the
warm and happy feelings.

I love you, my sweet little baby, **Baby**. Everyone starts out being a baby, and they grow to be big. Once I was a baby just like you. Then I grew and I grew and I grew. You will grow to be a (woman/man) someday. But for a short time you will be my little (girl/boy).

Share with Baby how it was for you when you were little. Describe your physical appearance. If you have photographs of yourself as an infant, show them to Baby. Describe how you looked like her. Tell her how you looked different from her. Let her know that it is good that she is unique and different from you and all others.

Twinkle, twinkle, little star,
How I wonder what you are!
Up above the world so high,
Like a diamond in the sky.

Nursery Rhyme

Soon you will be able to talk, **Baby**. What are you thinking, my beautiful baby? What words would you say if you could speak? What message do you have to share with me? Soon you will be able to share the secrets that are twinkling like stars inside your pretty head today.

Wisdom rests in the heart of him
who has understanding.

Proverbs 14:33

I treasure the person that you are becoming. I love you, **Baby**.

Do not be dogmatic, rigid, or judgmental towards Baby. If you never have kind words or loving arms available to her, she can never be happy or learn to love herself. If you ignore her needs and treat her in unkind ways, she will only learn self-hate. Be open and accepting of who she is, so she can be open and accepting of herself and who she is becoming.

Early to bed and early to rise
Makes a man healthy, wealthy, and wise.

Benjamin Franklin

I want to take good care of you because I love you, **Baby**. I am big, and I can give you the care that you deserve. Other people help care for you, too.

Describe each family member and tell what he does for Baby. You may want to include the community people like the pediatrician, the grocery clerk that stocks the baby food on the shelf, the bus driver that takes you to the park, etc. Let Baby know that he is important to lots of people besides you.

In all the world, there isn't another baby like you. Never has a baby exactly like you been born. You are unique and special in every way. You are perfectly you. No one else can ever be you, **Baby**. I love you.

List things that make Baby uniquely himself. Describe hair and eyes and skin and all the things that make your baby special. Read the list to Baby.

There was a an old woman
Lived under a hill;
And if she's not gone,
She lives there still.

Nursery Rhyme

We are here together today. The path of my life has led me to you. It was a long road to get here where I am with you today. I am thankful for the chance to be your mother. I am glad that we are together today, **Baby**.

Fathers, do not provoke your children to wrath,
but bring them up in the training....
Ephesians 6:4

⇌╬⇋

I love you, **Baby**. You are precious to me, and I appreciate everything about you. Everything about you is just right.

Although your infant may not understand the actual meaning of your words, he can grasp their non-verbal messages. If you are disappointed that your baby was a girl when you wanted a boy, she will get that clear message without being told. Is there something about your baby that disappoints you? You may want to talk this over with someone, or at least give it some soul-searching thought. Remember, Baby deserves to be exactly who she is. Unconditional acceptance and wholehearted appreciation for her is the best way to say, "I love you."

Sticks and stones can break my bones,
But words can never hurt me.

Nursery Rhyme

You are important, **Baby**. Your happiness is paramount to me. I will try to remember to speak to you always in a positive way. You deserve to hear good things.

That old adage that words can never hurt is so wrong! Words can hurt more than sticks or stones. Kind words can create a whole day of joy and happiness. Critical or angry words can make life miserable for everyone. For healthy emotional growth, babies need to hear many positive messages each day.

Ask, and you will receive,
that your joy may be full.
John 16:24

You are precious and unique, **Baby**. You are special and deserve to be treated in a kind and loving way. I will always try to treat you the way you deserve to be treated.

Assure Baby each and every day that you want him,
and you will be there to meet his needs as he grows and
develops. Let him know that you will work hard to help
him in every way you know how.

....shall flourish like a palm tree,
He shall grow like a cedar....
Psalms 92:12

Baby, I love you more every day. My love for you will continue to grow as you grow.

Your words are extremely powerful. Positive affirmations will be the rich soil in which your child can grow strong and tall.

Little Miss Muffet
Sat on a tuffet,
Eating her curds and whey;
There came a spider,
And sat down beside her,
And frightened Miss Muffet away.

Nursery Rhyme

I like being your mother, **Baby**. You change every day, and your needs do, too. Soon you won't need me to feed you. Someday you will dress yourself and comb your own hair. Today I will do all of these things for you. I will meet all of your physical needs. I love you, **Baby**.

Did you know that curds and whey are a little like cottage cheese? This is a good rhyme to say when feeding Baby cottage cheese. Cottage cheese is a good alternative to baby food. So are mashed avocado and yogurt.

Fulfill my joy by being like-minded,
having the same love,
being of one accord, of one mind.

Philippians 2:2

This day may be filled with surprises for us, **Baby**. I will be open to feel the love that you give me. I will be quiet and gentle and let you communicate your love for me.

Allowing Baby to express her love is a way of communicating. If all of your time together is filled with your words, she may not have time to express herself. Be still and listen for her non-verbal voice. Something beautiful and marvelous may happen today. Expect a miracle!

Let each of you look out not only for his own interests,
but also for the interests of others.

Philippians 2:4

I will do my best for you today because I love
you, **Baby**. I have your best interests at heart. I
want the best for you no matter what.

Don't be hard on yourself if sometimes you don't feel
like meeting Baby's every need. You may have to push
beyond the tired feelings to a place where you don't
mind the hard work. Meet his needs with a strong
feeling of love and with willingness to go beyond the
negative feelings. Then you may find that you don't
mind the difficulties so much.

Today is Halloween. People dress up today and pretend to be things besides themselves. Would you like to dress up today? Would you like to be a cat or a mouse? Let's draw whiskers on you and look in the mirror. **Baby**, let's take photographs of you on your first Halloween.

⊶⊶⊷⊷

If children will be ringing your doorbell for treats tonight, be sure to remember how scary masks can be for an unsuspecting child. Discussing the holiday and traditions may ease some of the threat. Baby may enjoy it tremendously, or she may be frightened. Be sensitive to her special needs tonight.

I love all of you, **Baby**. You are exactly the way you should be. I treasure the opportunity to be your mother.

Can you imagine how warm and comforting it is for Baby to know that you accept her exactly the way she is? Do you know that she loves and treasures you in that same unconditional way? You're the most important person in the world to Baby. You are cherished by Baby, Mommy. Enjoy the glow of this love relationship.

As the Father loved me,
I also have loved you;
abide in my love.

John 15:9

I love you, **Baby**. I love you with an eternal, unconditional love. I love each unique part of your character and personality. I love each facet of the jewel that is you.

Feelings are our primary biological motivators. What Baby is feeling at any particular moment is his authentic reality. When you reinforce positive feelings for him, you are establishing a happy environment for his healthy emotional growth. When you treat him in gentle, loving ways, no matter what the weather is outside, inside he will feel warm and secure.

Jack and Jill went up the hill
To fetch a pail of water;
Jack fell down and broke his crown,
And Jill came tumbling after.

Nursery Rhyme

I love to share books with you, **Baby**. Books are wonderful! I am reading to you from a book right now. This book helps remind me every day how important you are to me. As you get older, you will read books and learn from them, too.

Let Baby see you reading daily. Make sure she has her own cloth or vinyl-covered books. Have you ever taken Baby to the library? If possible, take her to a library often. Giving her a love for books at an early age will be one of the best things you can teach her.

"Croak!" said the toad, "I'm hungry, I think;
Today I've had nothing to eat or to drink.
I'll crawl to a garden and jump through the pails,
And there I'll dine nicely on slugs and on snails."
"Ho, ho!" quoth the frog, "is that what you mean?
Then I'll hop away to the next meadow stream;
There I will drink, and eat worms and slugs too,
And then I shall have a good dinner like you."

Nursery Rhyme

⊹⇒◎⇐⊹

Your whole body is extraordinary, **Baby**! All the
parts of your body are wonderful and do a special
job. Let's look at your knees and elbows, **Baby**.
Here are your knees. Aren't they cute the way
they bend? Here are your elbows. They bend,
too. Someday you will be able to hop and jump.

Blessed are your eyes for they see....
Matthew 13:16

You have beautiful eyes, **Baby**! Let's look at your eyes today.

Hold up a hand mirror for Baby to see his eyes. Say, "See your beautiful eyes. Your eyes are (name color). Eyes are how we see the world." Play peekaboo with Baby. Show him that when your eyes are closed, you cannot see--sight comes from our eyes. Going for walks and discovering interesting things is a good way to teach your baby about his eyes. If it is cold outdoors, you don't have to take your walks outside. Take Baby for a walk inside a mall, an art gallery, library, or school. You can even take a walk inside your own home, and talk about interesting things you find. Celebrate Baby's eyes today.

Blessed are your....ears for they hear.
Matthew 13:16

You have cute ears that can hear sounds, **Baby**. Yesterday we looked at your eyes. Today we will look at your ears. Let's take a walk today and listen for new sounds.

Hold up a hand mirror, and point out Baby's ears. Say, "Ears are how we hear sounds." When you tell Baby about his ears, touch them and help him touch them too. Touch your ears, and let him feel yours. Whisper in Baby's ear. Talk about interesting sounds that you hear. Play soft music for your baby. Listen to the sounds he makes; tell him you hear his sounds with your ears. Let him know how extraordinary the sense of hearing is by your enthusiasm.

Soon we will celebrate Thanksgiving.
Thanksgiving is a holiday when families come
together to celebrate their good fortune. I am
very thankful for you. I love you, **Baby**.

---

*Describe how the day will be for you and Baby. If you
are going to be with extended family for Thanksgiving,
begin telling Baby about the gathering. If you have photographs of people who will be there, show them to her.
Leave the photographs handy so you can prepare her
for the special celebration. The anticipation of the
holiday can be exciting for Baby, too. And if a gathering
of many people may frighten her, you can relieve some
of her anxiety by reassuring her in the coming days. It
doesn't matter if she is too small to understand every
word you speak. A reassuring tone of voice will make
her feel safe, so talk to her about Thanksgiving.*

Clothe me with skin and flesh,
And knit me together with bones and sinews.
You have granted me life and favor....

Job 10:11,12

I love you exactly as you are, **Baby**. I will support your true nature. Just as you were born with your own will, you will deal with life in your own unique ways. I will not try to change you. I will allow you to be who you are.

> *To alter a person's true nature deprives him of his actualization. A characteristic that may seem undesirable to you, such as stubbornness, may become tenacity in your child's adulthood. It may be exactly what he needs to get him through medical school. Support your infant's strong natural tendencies even when they may be inconvenient to you as a parent. The Creator knew what He was doing when He fashioned Baby and put the two of you together.*

Baby, I love to hear you babble and make your own sounds. That is how you will learn to talk. Someday we will have conversations about things you choose to discuss.

Some believe that people live in their conversations. You can help Baby feel more alive and happy if you listen to her "talk" and respond with sounds. Listening to her demonstrates that you care about her. Using a rich vocabulary when speaking to Baby today will make learning to talk easier. For now, share "conversations" in her wordless language of love.

It is okay that you cannot do anything for yourself. I like to bathe and dress you, Baby. I like to take good care of you. Sometimes I get tired, but always I love you, **Baby**.

If caring for Baby gets to be too much for you sometimes, ask for help. People do not know that you need help unless you tell them. Do you have a family support system? Do you know mothers of small babies with whom you can exchange care-giving for an afternoon out? Can you afford a baby-sitter for a few hours several times a week? If you are not getting time to rejuvenate, think of a plan for providing this vital time for yourself, Mommy. Your well being is important, too!

Dull November brings the blast,
Then the leaves are whirling fast.

Nursery Rhyme

Your happiness is important to me. I will never leave you, no matter how the world changes around us. I am here to take care of you and meet your needs. I like being your mother. I love you, **Baby**.

There isn't anything magical in these words of affirmation. They are the same things you have said over and over to Baby. Just as you like to hear that someone loves you, even when you already know they do, so does Baby. You cannot tell your baby too many times that you love him and will never abandon him. Assuring him that he is safe and that you will be there until he is old enough to care for himself will be comforting.

Look how beautiful **Baby** is! Look at your pretty eyes. Look at your sweet face. You are extraordinary!

Does Baby show specific preferences for certain family members? Does she prefer to be with you and other familiar persons? That is a good indication that she is becoming more aware of others as individuals. She is developing her own sense of selfhood. Looking into a mirror will help her comprehend that she has a body separate from yours. She will soon form an image of how she looks and who she is as an individual.

You are smart, **Baby**! I will support you when you want to learn on your own. Today I will place you on a blanket in a safe place and let you explore with your eyes and body.

The more opportunities you give Baby to explore, the more confident he will grow in his own abilities. As your baby becomes mobile, he will need more and more time and space to discover new things. Don't imprison him in a playpen. Although playpens offer a safe haven when you cannot be there watching, it isn't a good idea to keep him locked away hour after hour. Playpen learning is minimal. Optimal learning happens when Baby is interacting with other human beings or has plenty of room for exploration.

Jack be nimble, Jack be quick,
And Jack jump over the candlestick.

Nursery Rhyme

You are beautiful, **Baby**. The muscles in your body grow stronger every day. As time goes by, you will be able to do more and more things with your beautiful body.

After you dress Baby, show her how pretty she looks by placing her in front of a mirror. Let your baby see for herself how much she is growing. Play the game, How Big Is Baby? Ask the question, "How big is baby?" Then stretch your arms apart and say, "Sooooo big!" Soon she will be opening her arms when asked, "How big is Baby?"

And God is able to make all grace abound toward you....
through many thanksgivings.

II Corinthians 9:8,12

I am thankful that I will spend Thanksgiving Day with you, **Baby**. Thanksgiving Day is coming soon. You will taste some new foods on that special day. You will have fun.

Even if Baby isn't eating solid foods yet, he can taste the flavor of some traditional Thanksgiving Day foods. Name some of the foods that Baby may experience for the first time: jellied cranberry sauce, mashed potatoes, pumpkin pie filling. Describe some of the traditional foods that your family shares each year. Traditions are important. You will be starting a lifelong ritual for Baby this Thanksgiving.

"Yaup, yaup, yaup!"
Said the Frog, as it splashed about;
"Good neighbors all,
When you hear me call,
It is odd that you do not come out."

Nursery Rhyme

I am glad we will share time together today,
Baby. I enjoy being with you. I know you enjoy
being with me, too. When you call to me, I will
come to you.

*Take time to BE with Baby. Stop your mind from
racing. Be still, and enjoy precious memories you have
already shared. Relax. Enjoy the touch of the miracle
child in your arms.*

My mother, and your mother,
Went over the way;
Said my mother, to your mother,
It's a chop-a-nose day.

Nursery Rhyme

>‹

Your arms and hands are becoming stronger every day, **Baby**. Someday you will be big enough to throw a ball, dress yourself, play a musical instrument, and do other extraordinary and fun things. I will be there to applaud when you learn all of these new things. I love you, **Baby**.

An apple pie, when it looks nice,
Would make one long to have a slice,
But if the taste should prove so, too,
I fear one slice would scarcely do.
So to prevent my asking twice,
Pray, Mamma, cut a good large slice.

Nursery Rhyme

❄

I am very proud that I will be able to take you to the Thanksgiving Day dinner, and let everyone see how beautiful you are. The whole family is anxious to see you. They all love you, too, **Baby**.

You are beautiful, **Baby**. Look at the color of
your skin. It is (name the color). **Baby**, you
have beautiful skin. Look at the color of your
hair. You have pretty hair. You have beautiful
eyes. Your eyes are (name color). You are many
very beautiful colors.

*By the end of the seventh month, Baby will probably
have developed full color vision. Show Baby his hair in
a hand mirror. Talk about the beauty of his skin, hair,
eye colors. Let him know that he is a beautiful rainbow
of colors.*

I love you, **Baby**, even when you do not get what you want. I acknowledge that you want things that you cannot have. I will respectfully allow you to express your anger by letting you cry when you cannot have something you want. At the same time, you will not always get what you want. I know what is best for you.

Don't spank or punish Baby when she expresses nega-tive feelings. Allow her the gift of expressing all of her emotions. When she gets older and understands, you can teach her acceptable ways of displaying anger, impatience, frustration, and rage. For now, relax in the knowledge that she is expressing feelings in the only way she knows how--tears and tantrums.

Hello, **Baby**. Welcome awake. Do you want to talk? Do you like the telephone? Do you want to listen to the telephone? Let's play telephone.

If Baby is old enough, he probably likes to listen or even babble into the telephone receiver. Call someone, and let Baby hear a familiar voice. Even if he is too young to understand, the person at the other end of the receiver will enjoy a "conversation" with Baby. You can extend Baby's world and include extended family members with the telephone.

You are beautiful, **Baby**! Look at your cute little hands and feet. You have tiny fingers and toes. Each finger has a fingernail. Sometimes I have to trim them. Look at your pretty little toenails. We have to trim them, too.

Baby's nails will grow fast and may need to be trimmed at least once each week. Use a soft emery board or baby nail clippers. If Baby squirms when you trim her nails, try trimming them while she is sleeping.

"Yaup, yaup, yaup!"
Said the Frog; "it is charming weather
We'll come and sup,
When the moon is up,
And we'll all of us croak together."

Nursery Rhyme

You are curious, **Baby**. I love to watch your darting eyes as you discover new things. Being curious is how you learn. It is good to be curious.

To Baby, everything is new and exciting. It is a wonderful time when infants begin to look around and take in the world. Every new adventure is a celebration. Observe the world through Baby's eyes, and rejoice with him. Show him the magical things on the planet like frogs, full moons, and icicles. Try to find one new object each day to show and discuss with him.

Here am I, little jumping Joan,
When nobody's with me, I'm always alone.

Nursery Rhyme

I love to hug you, **Baby**. You love to get hugs from me. Hug. Hug. Hug. One, two, three. I'll hug you and you hug me. When we are not together, I will love you still.

Being alone is painful for some children. But you can teach Baby that being alone is okay. If she sees that you can be alone and quiet and entertaining yourself with a book or in a quiet way, she will learn that this is a good thing. If the television, radio, or people are always around you, buzzing and making noise, Baby may accept noise and confusion as how life should be. Provide a chaos-free, quiet place for Baby to relax, learn, and grow.

I like the way you are growing. You are growing in many different ways. Your body is growing, and your brain is growing, too. You are learning new things every day. You are a smart baby, **Baby**.

If you have questions about Baby's emotional or physical development, talk to your pediatrician. Don't waste energy worrying. Get an answer, and then relax and enjoy watching Baby grow.

For now you number my steps.
Job 14:16

Thank you for being who you are. I love you, **Baby**. I love watching you taking "steps" in your development.

Thank yourself for being who you are, too, Mommy. Each successful step you take in mothering will empower you and give you courage to take additional steps. You don't have to know everything today. Each day you will learn what you will need to know for the next day. Rest assured in the timing of the universe.

Sometimes you may not feel like being cuddled, and you might want time to be alone. Some days you might need more hugs than usual. I will try to be open to what you want and contribute to your comfort the best way I know how because I love you, **Baby**.

Don't be concerned if Baby has wide changes in temperament. It is normal for some babies to have mood swings. Just like you, she will have her up days and down days. Be sensitive to her moods and comfort Baby, but do not take them personally.

I accept all of you unconditionally. I welcome you to the world. You are a joy, **Baby**.

Remember that Baby loves you with an unconditional love also. You don't have to be the most beautiful or the most intelligent or the most anything. Baby loves you not because of anything you do but because you are his Mommy.

Miss Jane had a bag, and a mouse was in it,
She opened the bag, he was out in a minute.

Nursery Rhyme

I love to play with you, **Baby**. Today we can play together. Do you want to play a game?

Although Baby will have her own toys, many times children prefer to play with safe household objects such as plastic cups, spoons and utensils, small pillows and blankets, cardboard boxes and empty food containers, and unbreakable objects with unique shapes and bright colors. Being creative can extend the amount of learning aids Baby can experience and save you buying expensive toys. So look around the house to see what you can find for Baby's entertainment.

You are real, **Baby**. You are one of the most real and important things in my life. I love you. I will always love you. When we are both adults, and I am old and gray, I will still be your mother, and you will still be my son/daughter.

Growing up doesn't happen all at once. You become. It takes a long time. Be especially patient with Baby and yourself today.

❤ DECEMBER 1

Christmas comes but once a year,
And when it comes it brings good cheer.

Nursery Rhyme

This is the month of (Christmas/Hanukah). This is a season of holiday gift giving, making memories, and spending special times with the family. Today I am thankful for the gift of you in my life, **Baby**.

The traditions you observe this month will depend upon your religious beliefs. But any way you choose to celebrate the holidays, it will be Baby's first and a very special one for both of you. Resolve to make it relaxing and joy-filled.

I'll sing you a song,
Though not very long.

Nursery Rhyme

▸─┼◆▸─O─◂┼─◂

Baby, everything is okay. There is no hurry. Today we can sit quietly and breath deeply. We can stop and not be hurried just because the world around is quickening. We can hum a quiet tune especially for you.

> *Take time to slow down and explain things to Baby. If the world seems hurried to you this month, think of how chaotic it must be for your baby. Reassure yourself and Baby that it will soon return to a slower pace. In January, together you will settle back into a more quiet routine.*

You are the best gift in the world. I love you,
Baby. Do you want to play a Christmas wrapping paper game?

*Show Baby some brightly colored wrapping paper.
(Watch that she doesn't put it in her mouth.) Say,
"This is wrapping paper. Do you want some to crinkle
and throw around? People wrap presents in this shiny
stuff and tie them with bows." Use Christmas ribbons
to tie bows or Christmas bells on your baby's shoes.
Loosely wrap her hand or foot, and tell her that she is
the greatest gift in the world.*

❤ DECEMBER 4

I am so delighted to spend Christmas with you, **Baby**. Because you are here, this will be a very special Christmas. I will take photographs, so when you get older you can see your first Christmas.

Show Baby bright red and green objects. Do you have a peppermint stick for him to taste or a bayberry candle to smell? You and Baby can play holiday games together. Show him photographs of other Christmases that your family has shared. When you bake Christmas cookies, let him watch. Talk about the Christmas aromas in the kitchen. Christmas is a great time to stimulate all of your baby's senses.

Little boy blue, come blow your horn;
The sheep's in the meadow, the cow's in the corn.
Where's the little boy that looks after the sheep?
He's under the haystack, fast asleep.

Nursery Rhyme

You are safe, **Baby**. This house is your home. It is a good place for you to play. I want you to have freedom in our house to explore safely.

There are many things that you can do to make your house a safer place for Baby to explore: Place soft cushions of assorted colors, shapes, and sizes around on the floor so that she can move over and around them. Replace cleaning products under the kitchen sink with safe objects for her to discover and play with. Gate any stairways or doors that lead into rooms which contain dangerous objects. Make as much area of the house safe for baby as possible while making sure she cannot enter the unsafe parts.

I wonder what dreams of sugar plums are
dancing in your head. I hope your dreams are
sweet. You deserve sweet dreams. You are my
sweet dream, **Baby**.

*Read or recite the story, The Night Before Christmas, to
Baby. Play Christmas carols for him. Talk to him about
all of the sounds of Christmas: ho, ho, ho's, bells, carols,
etc.*

♥ DECEMBER 7

I love you, **Baby**. I offer my arms as a soft com-
forter for you. Wrapped safely in my warm love,
you can grow to be who you are meant to be. I
give you the gift of my support in fulfilling your
destiny.

═╬╬═

*One of the greatest gifts that you can give Baby is the
chance to become all that she is meant to be, not what
you want her to be. Today be open to who she is.
Watch for all of the signs of who she is becoming.
Nourish and guide, but don't prune branches and turn
her into a bonsai of the person she is meant to be.
Rejoice for the opportunity of sharing this tiny person's
beginning.*

Hush thee, my baby,
Lie still with your daddy,
Your mammy has gone to the mill
To grind you some wheat,
To make you some meat,
And so my dear baby lie still.

Nursery Rhyme

I love you, **Baby**, and I will always listen for your voice calling to me. I am going to put you in your bed now. Then I will leave. I will be in the next room doing (name the activity). I will be nearby where I can hear you if you cry out for me.

Practice leaving Baby in a safe place for just a moment or two at first. Extend the time gradually. Each time you leave the room, tell him where you are going and what you are planning to do. Tell your baby that you will be back soon and that you will be able to hear him calling to you. This will give him practice being separated from you.

❤ DECEMBER 9

And when there was a great silence,
he spoke to them....
Acts 21:40

I can love you even when I do not tell you,
Baby. Today we will sit in silence. I will show
you through my example that it is important to
be still. Today I give you the gift of silence.

*In silence we calm our mind and silence the ego. We
can discover who we are. Show Baby, through your
example, that sitting quietly can be a pleasant experience. Seeing you being still will be relaxing for her and
set a lifelong standard for a quality existence.*

Baby, you will get new toys this holiday season. It will be fun to shop for you. It will be nice to watch you playing with your new toys.

Be sure to check all new toys that Baby receives this holiday. Make sure that they are safe. Are there any small, loose pieces that Baby can put in his mouth? Are there any sharp edges? Watch how your baby plays with each toy to be sure that it is appropriate.

Cold and raw the North winds blow,
Bleak in the morning early,
All the hills are covered with snow,
And winter's now come fairly.

Nursery Rhyme

I will keep you safe and secure. With a smile, I will share the joy of the moment with you, **Baby**. In my arms, I will keep you warm and snug through cold winds, bleak mornings, and all the snowy, wintry days ahead.

You are loved by many, **Baby**. There are people besides me who love you and like to meet your needs.

———•━•━•———

Name family members and friends that help care for Baby. Extend Baby's world by asking family members to assist you in meeting her needs. Siblings are usually less jealous of a new baby if they are actively involved in the care-giving. Learning to delegate Baby's care to others will give you time to rest and meet your own needs.

There was a man, and his name was Dob,
And he had a wife, and her name was Mob,
And he had a dog, and he called it Cob.
And she had a cat, called Chitterabob.

Nursery Rhyme

I smile to tell you that you are safe with me. I smile because you make me feel happy. I smile at you, **Baby**, to tell you how much I love you. I am pleased to be with you.

Currahoo, currahoo, (sound a dove makes)
Love me, and I'll love you!
Nursery Rhyme

Your cooing sounds remind me of a dove's song. Your laughter is like the tinkling of a wind chime. Your babble voice is like a bubbling brook. All of your sounds are music played upon the strings of my heart. I love all of your voices, **Baby**.

Imitate some of the sounds you hear Baby making. Let him imitate the sounds you make. Play echo games. When you listen, you are sending him the message that what he has to say is important.

The North Wind does blow,
And we shall have snow,
And what will poor Robin do then?
He will hop to a barn,
And to keep himself warm,
Will hide his head under his wing,
Poor thing!

Nursery Rhyme

❖⟾⟾❖

You are healthy, **Baby**. It is good to feel strong and be healthy. Exercise is good for you. Do you want to exercise and stretch your legs and arms?

You can emphasize how important it is to exercise early with Baby by setting an example. Say, "Lie here on your back, and I will help you exercise your legs and arms. Stretch, pull, push. Does that feel good?" Does Baby ever see you exercising, running, or doing aerobics? If you aren't exercising three times a week, think about starting an exercise program for yourself. The more fit you are, the happier mother you will become. The happier mother you are, the happier Baby is. It is a magical circle of love.

❤ DECEMBER 16

It is good to have fun, **Baby**. Holiday decorations are pretty. Would you like to go somewhere and look at the decorations? I will take you on an outing (state when) and let you see the lights and trees and trimming. It is fun to see the decorations.

Since weather may not permit outdoor outings in many parts of the country, arrange to take Baby to a shopping mall or other indoor place that has decorations. Talk to him about all of the new colors, smells, and objects that he sees. Let Christmas be a visual feast.

I am always proud of you. Like Thanksgiving, the Christmas holiday is a time to be with family. This year we will get to see family members. They love seeing your beautiful face, **Baby**.

Holiday gatherings can be noisy and even frightening for babies. Ease the stress of big crowds by explaining to Baby ahead of time what to expect. Emphasize that the people she will be seeing are family and friends and that they all share in your love for her.

On the twelfth day of Christmas,
My true love sent to me
Twelve lords a-leaping,
Eleven ladies dancing,
Ten pipers piping,
Nine drummers drumming,
Eight maids a-milking,
Seven swans a-swimming,
Six geese a-laying,
Five gold rings,
Four calling birds,
Three French hens,
Two turtle-doves, and
A partridge in a pear-tree.

Nursery Rhyme

❦

I like listening to you, **Baby**. I like the songs you sing. Do you like holiday music? Do you want to hear some holiday songs? You can sing, too.

Play holiday music for Baby. Sing simple holiday songs instead of lullabies when putting him to sleep. Do you have a favorite Christmas carol? Tell Baby that it is your favorite song and play or sing it to him often.

I like to bathe you and keep you nice and clean. Do you like your bath? I like you, **Baby**. I like to see the bubbles on your belly. I like to see the water foam when you slap it with your little fist. Taking a bath is fun, **Baby**.

Do you bathe baby in the morning or evening? Some mothers feel that bathing early in the day is better because it washes away overnight diaper residue. Others prefer bathing their baby in the evening just before bedtime, because it may help Baby relax. You will have to experiment to see what time of the day is best for bathing.

Chill December brings the sleet,
Blazing fire and Christmas treats.

Nursery Rhyme

I love you, **Baby**. I love the days we are spending together. You are most precious to me. Your love warms me like a blazing fire. Your smile is a sweet Christmas treat.

> When you feel anxious or overly tired from the hard work of mothering, remember, no one will ever think you are as wonderful as your infant thinks you are right now. This is a marvelous time to be with your child. At no other time during her development will the two of you be quite this close.

Nestle there, my lovely one!
Press to mine your velvet cheek;
Sweetly coo, and smile, and look,
All the love you cannot speak.

Nursery Rhyme

I love your sweet coo, your smile, and your expressive eyes. I love the way you love me with your smiling face, **Baby**. I love the way you look, **Baby**, and I love the way you are.

Lulla, lulla, lullaby,
Softly sleep, my baby;
Lulla, lulla, lullaby,
Soft, soft, my baby.
Nursery Rhyme

You are my dream come true, **Baby**. Your presence in my life has made me very happy. You are the best holiday present ever.

See Baby as the precious gift that she is, and remember all of the positive, healthy, and nourishing gifts you have generously given her. You are doing a good job, Mother. Pat yourself on the back. You are a wonderful gift to Baby, too.

Baby, you can trust me to meet your needs. I am here and open to all of you. I am listening to your cries to hear what it is that you need from me. You can trust my love for you.

❖

A basic sense of trust is a deep holistic feeling. If Baby can learn to trust others, he can learn to trust himself. Children learn trust from trustworthy care-givers. If your care-giving is consistent and your love predictable, Baby will grow to trust others, too.

And she brought forth her first-born Son,
and wrapped Him in swaddling cloths,
and laid Him in a manger,
because there was no room for them in the inn.

Luke 2:7

This moment of holding you is perfect. It is with joy that I shelter you and keep you safe. Because of you, I share the joy that was Mary's when she gave birth in the stable two thousand years ago. I love you, **Baby**.

For there is born to you this day
in the city of David a Savior,
who is Christ the Lord.

Luke 2:11

➤❖

I love you on this Christmas Day, **Baby**. I look forward to sharing the day with you. Having you share my Christmas will make it more special than it has ever been before. I am glad you are here. Finally!

*Mary treasured up all these things
and pondered them in her heart.*

Luke 2:19

I love you. It was very special celebrating the holidays with you, **Baby**. I am glad you are my Baby. We will share many holidays in the years to come, and someday I will treasure my memories of your baby days.

> If the holiday was especially hectic and tiring, take the day to recuperate. Can you nap? Can you stay home and curl up in front of a fire? Can you take a long walk without Baby? Try to find some time to reflect on some of the holiday highlights.

You have a special little self. You have your own thoughts, feelings, wants, needs, and sensations within your body. I will support your being all of who you are and encourage you to feel all that you are feeling. All of you is okay, **Baby**.

Is Baby a little bored now that the quickened Christmas days have ended? Does she require a bit more attention? As she gets older, she may need more and more attention until she gets old enough to entertain herself. Soon the weather will be warm, and you can take her for walks and outings. Today, cocoon in the here-and-now and experience exactly how it is. Next December, Baby will be older and very different. Today is perfect for now.

Being your mother is a pleasure. Loving you makes me very happy. I love you, **Baby**.

Love and mothering are an important part of what makes life wonderful. But Baby doesn't have to be your only source of pleasure. Make a list of the pleasant things that you do other than mothering. Do you often celebrate these now that you are a mother? Is your life balanced? You will enjoy caring for him more if it isn't the only thing that you do.

I am real with you. You are real with me. The truth of our love is pure and divine. I love you, **Baby**.

Being authentic with Baby will teach her how to be real and how to accept her true self. If Baby is encouraged to be real, then she will be free to be creative and discover, explore, and complete her emotional growth and development.

I will use a gentle voice and pleasant facial expressions to show you my love today. I want to give you many positive experiences because I love you, **Baby**.

Remember that Baby is storing all of the sensory information that he experiences as good feelings or bad feelings. Although you may not be aware of it, you are creating neurological imprints every time you deal with Baby. All of his sensory experiences are coded by auditory, olfactory, or gustatory anchors. For example, if you wear a perfume that smells like roses, and hold Baby lovingly, you are imprinting his brain in a positive way. For the rest of his life, the fragrance of roses may trigger a certain feeling of security.

Man is like a breath;
His days are like a passing shadow.
Psalm 144:4

Today is the last day of this year. I am glad you were in my life this year. We will have many years together. You are changing every day. It will be wonderful to be near to watch you grow in the coming years. I love you sincerely, **Baby**.

Are you keeping a journal? Baby is changing so quickly. A few sentences jotted down in a journal may someday provide a wonderful milestone log for Baby. See the Milestones that follow. You may want to include each of these in your journal. Resolve to keep a Baby Journal next year and take lots and lots of photographs. The year ahead will be extraordinary for both you and Baby!

❤ MILESTONES

First Smile

Date: _____   Response to: _____
Age:_____

Raised Head and Chest while Lying on Stomach

Date: _____   Comments:
Age:_____

Grasped and shook hand toy

Date: _____   Comments:
Age:_____
What was the toy?_____

Said first word

Date: _____   What was the word?_____
Age:_____   Comments:

Assumed a sitting position

Date: _____   Comments:
Age:_____

First tooth

Date: _____   Which tooth was it?_____
Age:_____   Comments:

Crawled forward on stomach

Date: _____   What did he crawl toward?_____
Age:_____   Comments:

Assumed hands-and-knees position

Date: _____   Comments:
Age:_____

368

Crept on hands and knees

Date: _____   Comments:
Age:_____

Walked holding something for support

Date: _____   Comments:
Age:_____

Shook head for "No"

Date: _____   Comments:
Age:_____

Used fingers to feed himself

Date: _____   Comments:
Age:_____

Said "Dada" (or other word for Father)

Date: _____   Exact sound made:_____
Age:_____   Comments:

Said "Mama" (or other word for Mother)

Date: _____   Exact sound made:_____
Age:_____   Comments:

Stood momentarily without support

Date: _____   Comments:
Age:_____

Took first steps

Date: _____   Comments:
Age:_____

❤ GROWTH GRAPH WEIGHT IN KG

13 KG

12 KG

11 KG

10 KG

9 KG

8 KG

7 KG

6 KG

5 KG

4 KG

3 KG

MO   birth 1 2 3 4 5 6 7 8 9 10 11 12

❤ GROWTH GRAPH LENGTH IN CENTIMETERS

42 cm
44 cm
46 cm
48 cm
50 cm
52 cm
54 cm
56 cm
58 cm
60 cm
62 cm
64 cm
66 cm
68 cm
70 cm
72 cm
74 cm
76 cm
78 cm
80 cm
82 cm

MO   birth   1   2   3   4   5   6   7   8   9   10   11   12

♥ BABY'S PERSONAL IMMUNIZATION CHART

Date:
DTP   ___2 MO   ___4 MO   ___6 MO   ___15-18 MO
Date:
Polio   ___2 MO   ___4 MO   ___15-18 MO
Date:
TB Test   ___12-15 MO
Date:
Measles   ___15 MO
Date:
Mumps   ___15 MO
Date:
Rubella   ___15 MO

About the Author

Becky Daniel is a parent, teacher and writer, three distinctive yet interrelated professions. After graduating from California University at Long Beach, she taught kindergarten through eighth grade. When she began her family, she left the classroom to care for her first daughter, Amy, and to pursue a career in writing at home.

Now, the mother of three children: Amy, Sarah, and Eric, she writes and edits from her home in Orcutt, California. Over the past eighteen years she has authored dozens of educational activity books for Good Apple, Inc., and Shining Star. For twelve years she was editor of *Shining Star Magazine* and is now the editor of *New Day* Magazine.

She is also the author of a picture book, *Prince Poloka of Uli Loko*, a Hawaiian story for children. Her biographical sketch and a complete list of her books are featured in Volume 57 of *Something About the Author*.

About the Illustrator

Nancee McClure has been an illustrator and a developer of materials for children since 1975. After receiving a master's degree in art education, teaching school and working as art director for a publisher of educational materials she started her own company, Good Neighbor Press, Inc. Good Neighbor Press handles the development, illustration, and production of materials for young children and educators of young children.

She recently finished illustrations for a picture book, *Acorn Alone*, which was authored by her husband, Michael. Nancee and her family live in Colorado where they enjoy the benefits of small town living and beautiful surroundings.